Dancing With A Broken World

COPYRIGHT © Dr. Danny Griffin,
1st Edition April 2018
Printed in the United States of America

Dr. Danny Griffin
dwadegriffin@gmail.com
www.SpiritualMaintenance.org

Table of Contents

Dancing With A Broken World

ABOUT THE BLOGGER

Danny Griffin has been a friend of mine since 1955. It has been my privilege to witness his spiritual growth since his ministry began. In these latter years I have seen him move from religious correction and aimless denominationalism to real Christianity. His writings reflect a genuine down to earthiness that addresses the needs and hurts of humanity. His book _"Dancing With Broken Feet"_ and now _"Dancing With a Broken World,"_ go together in putting the pieces in place for those who need help. His writings are a style all his own; they are made to communicate, not to impress. Read as though you were listening to him speak. Feel the pathos and compassion in every chapter that comes from a man who has lived in the raw of life's experiences and emerged victoriously. Raised by a Godly pastor father and a teacher mother Danny brings to the written page wisdom predestined to be shared by many, concerning the love and grace of our Lord Jesus Christ and life choices!

Dr. George H. Harris

Baptist Ouachita University B.A. 1958, B.D. M.Div. Southwestern Baptist Theological Seminary.1965, D. Min. Luther Rice Theological Seminary-.- 1976 Honorary Degrees'- Ouachita Baptist University Doctor of Divinity-D.D> Grand Canyon University- Doctor of Literature – D.Litt.

I met Danny Griffin when we both lived in Magnolia, AR. Shortly thereafter I left Magnolia and moved to Lubbock, TX. I wrote a little book titled "The Glorious Return of Jesus Christ." Danny called expressing his appreciation for my writings. Since that time we have stayed in touch via phone and social media. Danny is a prolific writer and a great Bible scholar. He writes a regular blog that he publishes on social media. Having read several of his blogs I highly recommend his writings. He has written and published several books in which he shows great insight into human problems and offers solutions from his knowledge of God's Word. I have just finished reading his book titled "Dancing With Broken Feet" in which he discusses the problems caused by divorce. Danny shares how those who have experienced the tragedy of a divorce can pick up the pieces of a broken relationship and rebuild a meaningful life. I encourage anyone who needs spiritual help with life's problems to pick up one of Danny's books and find answers from God's Word that can speak to your life choices!

Dr. Jimmy Henry

Attended Jacksonville Baptist College 1952-1956: A.A. and Th.B. Degrees Attended Baylor University 1956-1950: B. A. Degree Attended North American Theological Seminary 1958-1964: B.D. and Th.M. Degrees Attended American Divinity School 1964-1968: Th.D. and Litt.D.Degrees. Pastored churches from 1954 to the present!

Danny has been a dear brother and friend for more than 40 years. He ministered to me back in the early 70's when I was aimless, seeking only to please myself - a rebel without a cause. For all these years he has been a beacon in the fog, always pointing the way to The Christ. He is the reason when I lack reason; he always offers insight and clarity in a BROKEN WORLD. I have spent my entire 39 years working in many computer technology disciplines for corporate America. I am neither a theologian nor a pastor, simply a believer in Christ who is walking down the road like everyone else. I can only say that I would have strayed far and deeper had it not been for my dear brother in Christ Danny Griffin. Thank you brother!

Don Cleveland II

Florida Bible College / NC State University Computer Science / Cloud Computing Technical Enablement & Sales

DEDICATION

This second book of the "DANCING WITH" series I dedicate to my faithful, loving, wife DIANE, our daughter, Elizabeth, and to Diane's parents, RALPH and DORIS FERRELL who ADOPTED me into their family unconditionally with love and care IN THIS BROKEN WORLD! Without them this series might never been written.

FOREWORD

These Blogs are from my Journal of Spiritual Maintenance. Over the years of my spiritual journey I moved away from programmed religion to a more personal, in-your-face concern for Biblical truth, Jesus Christ and shoe leather 24/7. My Mother was born in Texas and my Dad in North Carolina. My dad, grandfather and uncle were pastors. I belonged to a mobile family moving as my Dad's ministry took us different places during my childhood and teen years. It became my fate to always be the new boy. I was born in NY, lived in Ohio, Michigan, South Carolina, North Carolina, Florida, Arkansas, Texas, Kentucky and Indiana.

My Dad's ministry moved us to Belle Glade, Florida when I was in the 9th grade. I loved the people and my life there in the 50's. In my junior year my parents enrolled me in Hampden Dubose Academy in Zellwood, Florida. This was a Christian boarding school, where my life would undergo some major changes. Students from around the world and loving teachers introduced me to faith as a lifestyle. I moved from a religious veneer to a more honest look at my life. Teachers, speakers and students whose search for spiritual reality changed my life forever.

After high school I attended Furman University, Ouachita University, Trinity University, Southern Seminary and Trinity Seminary Bible College. Spiritual Maintenance Ministries was born by way of a newsletter, charting my personal growth and my struggle with Christianity vs. Jesus Christ. This was a struggle that would intensify in the 80's while teaching pastors in India. I also rediscovered C.S. Lewis when I stopped over in England to spend time with my son Tim, a student at Oxford. We spent time at the old home place of Lewis and the Eagle and Child Pub where Lewis and Tolkien would hang out daily to discuss their writings.

Thus, Spiritual Maintenance and Blogs became my way of sharing my journey, and "no agreement was ever required." Who I believed became more important than what I believed. Facebook was my ticket to reconnect with many friends I missed and also connect with new digital friends. It was like sitting on a neighbor's "internet front porch." The NEWSLETTER gave way to BLOGS as I found it a better way to communicate with people in my life. Spiritual Maintenance was never about sermons or lectures but a search for understanding and wisdom in a BROKEN WORLD filled with hurting people and CHOICES. I have met many new people through my

BLOGS, BLURBS and BOOKS. They have become my digital and intellectual family making my life richer. Welcome to the world of a BLOGGER confronting life's CHOICES!

INTRODUCTION

These blogs are digital conversations meant to deal with the hard realities and choices of life. No agreement required. Blogs are not sermons and lectures but a hard search into my life's journey. The spiritual slant is not an argument to be won but a search for truth that will alter life's meaning.

In the days of my youth we visited our neighbors, sat on their porches, churned ice cream, explored life's realities and shared the good, the bad and the ugly. Conversations were filled with small talk and serious discussions dealing with the hard issues of life. These were a form of loving not fighting, even when there were differing opinions.

When my son Tim was in Oxford, we would hang out at pubs after 6pm and relish the loud friendly conversations that filled the air. We have in these days often lost the art of conversation face to face. We have become addicted to digital communication, everyone with their own digital weapon. I too have joined the ranks of digital communicators and am daily challenged to find my way.

My Dad used to tell me that the written word was mightier than the sword. Thus, I have written BLOGS, BLURBS, and BOOKS which have caused me to wrestle with what is true, honest and life affirming in my brief time on the stage of life. The authority of Scriptures, GOD'S LOVE AND GRACE revealed in the person of JESUS CHRIST found me when I was confused about life and its meaning. My life, my conversations and my writings now deal constantly with the POWER-DRIVEN LIFE, empowered by JESUS CHRIST, His death, burial and resurrection. The BELIEVER is not about being good or bad but about being weak or strong. GOD'S PERFORMANCE on my behalf makes it possible for HIS PROVISION to become the constant and consistent resource for my daily journey and CHOICES. Those choices are no longer based on MY PERFORMANCE or RIGHTEOUSNESS but faith in HIS. Finally, the reason for my hope and joy is JESUS not ME-SUS!

JESUS!

We all live in a broken and angry world. My blogs are a continued search and struggle with the nature and character of God in a world of spiritual counterfeits, smoke and mirrors, and dog and pony shows. Thus, I return again and again to certain themes that challenge my daily world of CHOICES where cheap ritualized religion has often replaced the miracle and power of "Amazing Grace."

SCRIPTURE DECLARES:

> *"Oh the depth of the riches both of the wisdom and knowledge of God! For who has known the mind of the Lord, or who became His counselor? Or who has first given to Him that it might be paid back to Him again? For from Him and through Him and to Him are all things. To Him be glory forever. "He who has seen me has seen the Father;" (JESUS) "God highly exalted Him (JESUS), and bestowed on Him the name which is above every name, so at the name of Jesus every knee will bow, of those who are in heaven and on earth and under the earth, and that every tongue will confess that Jesus Christ is Lord, to the glory of God the Father." God is the great "I AM"! JESUS declared, "I AM THE WAY, THE TRUTH AND THE LIFE."*

He is for evermore! "In the beginning God CREATED." It is He we worship. His power is awesome. We glorify His name! The Father gave us

Jesus. His authority is over us. We are His servants. JESUS BORN OF A VIRGIN, DIED ON THE CROSS, WAS BURIED IN A STRANGER'S GRAVE, AND ROSE FROM THE DEAD FOR OUR SALVATION. GOOD NEWS!

ENEMY WITHIN!

The years of one's personal walk with the LORD is filled with highs and lows. It takes a lifetime of growing to overcome self-righteousness and false piety. A missionary told me once that the greatest problem he faced was other missionaries. Over the years I have been a problem to other believers as they are at times to me. We are all wired different and reveal warts and flaws. God's love, grace and forgiveness draws us in and carries us through the good, the bad and the ugly times.

It was Gandhi of India who said,

"I would be a Christian except for the Christians."

I probably have been one of those at times who has shut the door of grace in someone's face! Thus, in dealing with those who have shut me out of their lives because of my failings and insensitivity I have learned this little rap:

"He drew a circle that shut me out, a heretic, a rebel, a thing to flout, but love and I had the wit to win, we drew a circle to shut him in." (Markham)

Daily I must seek God's face in dealing with my brokenness, sinfulness and inability. I am often my biggest enemy. God and His love and grace are my greatest joy in making DAILY LIFE CHOICES!

MESSY WORLD!

Real life is really messy! When God found me and wrapped me in His love and forgiveness I was a mess. Daily I throw myself on the court of God's eternal love and grace because Jesus died on the CROSS in my place giving me the gift of His righteousness. He traded His mercy for my messy sinfulness. Life has not been perfect and at times messy still, but with His grace filling my life His joy overwhelms my brokenness. His power fills my heart and causes my feet to dance with meaning and purpose!

Thus, in this messy world I flee boldly into God's presence daily at the throne of grace always knowing that my Lord and Savior eternally opened that door for all who trust Him. We can moment by moment claim His life, death and resurrection as our very own! In this messy world Jesus is our only blessed hope. I would invite you to invite Him into your messy world today! CHOICES!

BEST DAYS!

Those were the best days of my life. In 1989 I had just returned from India with my teaching team, Dick Hill and Nap Clark. They were precious gifted men on a special mission teaching God's Word to village pastors and sharing the Gospel with multitudes. I had been invited back to Carolina Christian Ministries to help tie up some loose ends from the past. Mission India cemented acceptance of that invitation.

Returning proved to be the greatest challenge of my life as well as the greatest blessing. Precious people trusted Christ and were discipled. I prayed daily for hurting people, desiring to make a difference. God is good, and I am blessed, grateful for all who pray for me and forgave my failures.

These days are still the best days of my life. In the words of my Dad as a pastor for 65 years he declared:

> *"Between 70 and 90 were the best years of my life, not impressed with anybody and not trying to impress anybody, just being myself to God's Glory and his good"!*

Me too Pop! CHOICES MAKE A DIFFERENCE!

QUIET LIFE!

Scripture declares

> "...make it your ambition TO LEAD A QUIET LIFE, MIND YOUR OWN BUSINESS and WORK WITH YOUR OWN HANDS," and "BE READY TO GIVE A REASON OF THE HOPE WITHIN TO THOSE WHO ASK."

I grew up in a religious culture that reminded us weekly that we were to be aggressive in talking about God and the Gospel to everyone. Guilt stood at my door if I didn't, and thus as one, caught between "go and guilt," I did nothing. The idea was to share your faith with every human for fear they would die and go to hell, and it would be our fault.

As a young teenager I passed it off as church talk, meant only for full time preachers, missionaries and anyone else who would join those special "God's Pets," who were as folks would say, "on fire for God." My understanding of GRACE was weak and being a pastor's son, I was already strange enough to my "peer group," so I refrained from any "religious behavior" except church attendance. Many church members seemed to be just like me except on Sunday where "shoulda, woulda, coulda" was always a part of the human condition seeking to be religious.

At the age of sixteen God found me in my misery and frustration, trapped between the culture of my raising and the "if it feels good do it" lifestyle. It is not hard to guess where I landed. At that most needy time in my life God found me. My relationship to God was established by the work of Jesus Christ on my behalf. His death, burial and resurrection constituted a personal relationship, not a corporate religious connection.

My daily walk taught me to trust God's provision of love and grace, not my performance. Thus, MINDING my OWN business, living a QUIET LIFE and WORKING with my OWN HANDS, translated into the metaphors of SALT and LIGHT that JESUS used and were positive witnesses to GOD'S LOVE and GRACE. The QUIET LIFE is not a life of illusion and escape, but a life of absolute TRUST that God will bring into our lives those opportunities to share His love and grace. Such a relationship is a personal, intimate relationship, more WALK than TALK.

We as believers are GRACED messengers having been allowed to share God's life-giving message. HE gives the increase, doing HIS work in and through us, honoring HIS WORD as promised, to HIS glory and OUR good. THUS OUR REASONED HOPE IS A RESULT OF A FAITH CHOICE!

LAW AND ORDER!

We as individuals and society must have order in our lives. It is both a personal and corporate necessity for us to function and live our lives with meaning. At the heart of orderly living are the laws which govern and protect our freedoms and functions. Every part of life is governed by specific laws. Our Constitution is the primary document along with the Bill of Rights of America and makes us who we are. If we ever sacrifice these truths to the political whims of people with other agendas, we will no longer be America.

Freedom is never free and as a nation under the RULE OF LAW our daily lives are given order, definition and meaning. As believers we are also governed by spiritual laws given to us in God's Word and are empowered in our lives by the Holy Spirit. Listed here are some of our daily involvements governed by particular laws so as to live in order instead of chaos and disorder.

MATHEMATICS / PHYSICS / MUSIC / SPIRITUAL LIFE / BIOLOGY / ART / SCIENCE / MILITARY / GOVERNMENT / MEDICINE / EDUCATION / HUMANITIES / PHILOSOPHY / PSYCHOLOGY / HEALTH / ENGINEERING / GARDENING / COOKING / BOATING / CONSTRUCTION / FAMILY

Law – a consistent manifestation of a principle or behavior in the natural or supernatural realm, thus establishing an authority for defining or knowing anything. A demand based upon an authority that has the knowledge and power to demand a required response.

Order – to arrange and regulate those matters of reality so that a standard is set by which we can live in peace and security, and by which we can all be informed and protected from ourselves and others.

There are laws at work in everything in the universe, by which order and disorder, function and dysfunction can be determined. Spiritual Maintenance deals with the realm of the spiritual and the nature and character of God revealed to mankind so that we can know Him and know who we are because of who He is.

God has manifested Himself in a certain consistent manner by His acts and provisions for mankind, revealing His righteousness. His righteousness has to do with the absolute consistency and perfection of His character manifest in His creation and the laws of all things in His universe. He gives His righteousness as a gift out of the abundance of grace. When mankind fails to obey His laws and works contrary to His laws in both the natural and supernatural domains there is failure, confusion, and disorder.

God's ways are above and beyond our ways and "His law is perfect" bringing order, restoring the soul. Because the law of the Lord is perfect we are commanded by Jesus Christ to "seek first the kingdom of God and His righteousness and everything else will be added unto us." The purpose of God's law was to bring us to Christ. Scripture declares that the "law was given through Moses, grace and truth was realized through Jesus Christ" and we have received from God's fullness in His Son, "GRACE UPON GRACE." Scripture speaks of the "abundance of grace, the gift of His righteousness" in Jesus Christ. Truly God's law was perfected in Jesus Christ who came not to destroy the law but to fulfill it. God's law always reveals His love. His wisdom and His desire are to make us one with Him based on His grace not our works. It's all about Him not us. We are either outlaws or in-laws joined to Christ by His Love and grace, "joint heirs with Jesus Christ" on the basis of faith.

GOD'S LAW EQUALS GOD'S LOVE WHICH SETS US AT ONE WITH HIM AND APPLIES HIS WISDOM TO OUR LIVES. WE CANNOT FULFILL THE LAW, BUT IT DELIVERS US TO CHRIST WHOSE RIGHTEOUSNESS FULFILLS OUR OBLIGATION

TO THE LAW! We CHOSE GOD'S Provision not our Performance!

LOVE AND LOINS

"Stand therefore, having girded your LOINS with truth, and having put on the breastplate of righteousness."

Our SEXUALITY and SPIRITUALITY are gifts from our Designer Creator.

Scripture declares,

"In the beginning God created heaven and earth."

Our spirituality demands a NEW BIRTH so that it is disconnected from mankind's addiction to a religion of DO and FIX as an attempt to be good enough for God to love and honor.

Our SEXUALITY is a gift for the ultimate of pleasure and pain. One flows from mankind's great need to be loved and the other for the need of INTIMACY which often surrenders to the quick fix of intense pleasure without intimacy which bears us much pain. From birth both wonderful gifts can become corrupted. When void of meaning our LOINS seek pleasure without love or satisfaction, gaining only temporary physical relief. As believers, over a lifetime we confront both.

Thus, having experienced failure we seek a new direction. We will forever confront SPIRITUALITY

AND SEXUALITY, realities with which we will STRUGGLE till the day we leave this body. Spiritual hunger will only be satisfied with God's love and grace. A religion of good works cannot satisfy our brokenness and sin. It is God's gift and He alone can fix us. Jesus died, was buried and rose from the dead to give us REAL LIFE!

Our sexuality seeks a lasting home where it lives apart from threat and hurt. Marriage was God's answer even as it confronts potholes and personal warts. Out of its LOINS "girded with truth" come family, and under self-control, a fruit of the Spirit, comes strength and power.

Both King David and Solomon dramatized the desperation of "broken sexuality" as do we in the war of our minds in an "overly pleasure hungry world" starving for LOVE, GRACE AND ETERNAL FORGIVENESS! I have walked down both MEAN STREETS over my lifetime and am driven to declare VICTORY IN JESUS only.

As believers, we daily confront the weakness of the flesh and the strength of God's grace till we go to be with the Father. As Simon Peter said to Jesus when confronted with a CHOICE to leave, "YOU HAVE THE WORDS OF LIFE, THERE IS NO WHERE ELSE TO

GO"! THE CHOICE IS OURS!

MEAT-ING TIME!

Perhaps the gathered modern meetings, called church, are musical presentations with sermons and lectures. Discipleship requires "dinner table" sharing with each believer equally involved in answering questions and questioning answers while each ministers to the other. It does not require a professional to search the Scriptures.

Elders, meaning older and more experienced should be given great respect, as well as men and women who have served faithfully, spoken of in the New Testament as elders, deacons and ministers. The older men should teach the younger men and the older women the younger women as both men and women teach equally from their growth in grace and overflow of walking in the Spirit. It is at this point that those who have walked faithfully among us through life's good, bad and ugly truly become to the body of Christ, facilitators for the younger and less experienced believer.

Indeed, it is obvious that the Holy Spirit of God is the communicating voice of God who addresses the inner man as we ponder, muse and meditate upon God's Word and His nature and character. The Holy Spirit is indeed the quiet voice who speaks to us thru

Scripture which is "God breathed." He addresses our inner man as He did to Elijah of old in a "whisper."

Then we learn in great humility to address one another in quiet tones of love and grace one to another as we read scripture, exhort each other as when our moms called us to the dinner table with love and anticipation of a love feast prepared by her hands. Thus we exhort each other to come and dine from God's Word to feed our hungry inner man.

Yelling and hollering and noisy drama is not our need, but a quiet love feast among brothers and sisters at God's table where we "bear one another's burden." Therefore we share in the joy of a meal where the cook is just one of the eaters, rejoicing in the nurture of the food shared by eager eaters.

The gatherings of many these days are in a noisy hall among repetitive words set to melody, while we sit in rows behind each other looking at "ears and rears" listening to a talking head. At the dinner table we settle in for the joy of the food, and the thrill of conversation dealing with life's many realities. This indeed is the music of heaven as the, "Word of Christ dwells richly in us" as food for the soul, and we bless one another with "spiritual songs and psalms," loving conversation filled with laughter and tears flowing from the heart with "thankfulness in our hearts to God"!

Here at each gathering at the table we eat of God's food as the Holy Spirit whispers God's blessing to each at the presence of food and blessing, looking into each other's eyes and speaking freely, answering questions and questioning answers. Each precious soul as important as the other, all equal at the table of blessing, with love and prayers. SHARING THE BREAD OF LIFE AND THE MEAT OF THE WORD, DRINKING LIVING WATER! FULFILLING CHOICES!

HOPE!

Reaching my teens I found religion interesting and emotional but predictable, boring and overly judgmental producing guilt and failure. I was a superficial follower of JESUS, having been baptized and joined the church at an early age, a pastor's son. My junior year in high school found me enrolled by my parents in a Florida boarding school, based on academics and the Bible. After a close encounter with expulsion and my Dad's "better not" I began facing my lack of spiritual direction. One of my teachers revealed her prayers on my behalf.

My over familiarity with church-oriented religion, its politics and routine caused me to make promises many times out of guilt. In a real sense it had insulated me from dealing with my own spiritual need. Later in my 16th year I had a "HELLO JESUS" moment that drives my LIFE until this day. Well-meaning people had asked me for years, had I "found JESUS," had I "given my heart to Him" and did I know "I would go to heaven" if I died. Walking aisles, raising my hand, saying canned prayers and memorizing scriptures had become for me a religious work offering little help or HOPE of changing my insecurities and inadequacies.

After my conversation with Mrs. Hill one day at HDA I began to search the Scripture and discover a new strength, zeal and HOPE for living. My religion of try hard to be good had been captured by SCRIPTURES that declared me RIGHTEOUS, NOT BASED ON MY PERFORMANCE BUT GOD'S PROVISION. AMAZING GRACE! This became my KNOW SO HOPE! The dictionary defines HOPE as an EXPECTATION OF FULFILLMENT and I define it as follows:

H *HEART* – We are a letter of Christ written on our HEARTS. This letter of truth is not written with ink, nor on tablets of stone but with the Spirit of the living God on tablets of the HEART. Thus, our HOPE is written in our individual personal lives for us to know and the world to see our good works and glorify the Father. It is not of human origin nor human performance, but a gift of GOD'S RIGHTEOUSNESS PROVIDED BY HIS ABOUNDING GRACE! HOPE'S HOME!

O *OBTAIN* – On the basis of faith I now am promised to attain resurrection from the dead, not that I have now OBTAINED it or am perfect already but on a journey of faith. Flesh and blood will not inherit the kingdom of God for I have not yet become immortal and without corruption but will put them on when I leave this mortal, corrupt body for the other side, having put my trust in Jesus the way, the truth and the life by faith alone and sealed by the HOLY SPIRIT of promise to the day of REDEMPTION. HOPE'S SECURITY!

P *PEACE* – We have PEACE WITH GOD through our Lord Jesus Christ obtaining our introduction into His grace by faith. Therefore, we boast in the HOPE of the glory of God. The PEACE OF GOD provides us our entrance into the PEACE WITH GOD which passes all understanding. HOPE'S PEACE!

E *ENDURE* – HOPE is a faith reality, a saving HOPE, a good HOPE, a sure HOPE, a living HOPE, a purifying HOPE, and a comforting HOPE, given by God. It is affirmed in the SCRIPTURES, made an eternal reality signed and sealed by the blood of JESUS CHRIST ON THE CROSS finally DELIVERED by HIS RESURRECTION FROM THE DEAD. I now stand SEALED TILL THE DAY OF REDEMPTION.

IN HOPE I HAVE BEEN SAVED; FOR HOPE THAT IS SEEN IS NOT HOPE, FOR IN HOPING FOR WHAT WE DO NOT SEE BY ENDURANCE WE WAIT PATIENTLY FOR IT. One of my favorite hymns I have played often says it all: MY HOPE IS BUILT ON NOTHING LESS THAN JESUS BLOOD AND

RIGHTEOUSNESS.... ON CHRIST THE SOLID ROCK I STAND ALL OTHER GROUND IS SINKING SAND. HOPE'S TRUTH!

MY WAY OR GOD'S WAY?

MY WAY OR THE HIGHWAY! Scripture declares that the JUDGES of Israel did what was RIGHT IN THEIR OWN EYES. As a result, Israel drifted from her calling and purpose.

My Mom reminded me every time I went off with a group of people for a time of fun or serious pursuit,

"Remember who you are."

She simply wanted me to remember my raising and instruction before others.

As believers we have been set free from religion and self-righteousness by our salvation and freedom in Jesus Christ. That personal relationship over a lifetime changes how we think and live. We have no righteousness of our own, but the ABUNDANCE OF GOD'S GRACE GIVES US THE GIFT OF HIS RIGHTEOUSNESS. There is no room for self-righteousness or "goody two-shoes" arrogance. We must grow in His grace into a true humility manifesting a servant's heart. Time and again each one of us who believes God has wasted life opportunities on self-serving pursuits; doing what is right in our eyes.

As a loving parent, God disciplines us as He did

Israel by giving us over to our own choices which always come back to haunt us. We need daily to pray the words of King David as we confront our daily self-serving and sinfulness, RESTORE UNTO US THE JOY OF OUR SALVATION. Sin and injurious behavior may be fun for a season, but when all is said and done it has a short shelf life. Our thinking and choices are often "me" centered leading to personal pain and struggle.

Our lives are made up of a sum of CHOICES, the good, the bad and the ugly. Doing what is right in my own eyes affects my fellowship with God and man. That is a lonely place to be. My daily prayer is "God deliver me today from Danny Griffin," and if possible deliver others from him also. Finally, we must learn to surrender our will and way to God, leaning not on our own understanding but trusting in God and His Word. THIS TAKES A LIFETIME OF KNOWING AND GROWING. THUS, THE CHOICE IS HIS WAY OR MY WAY!

NEEDY?!

As a kid I would hear the adults sing a song that declared, "Not my sister, not my brother but me Oh Lord, standing in the NEED OF PRAYER." The Scriptures declare that we don't know how to pray as we ought, but the HOLY SPIRIT makes known our needs with unutterable groanings, knowing both the will of God and our need.

Daily as I come and go I routinely pray in behalf of people's NEEDINESS! The one thing common to all mankind is NEEDINESS. Thus, we never miss the mark in praying for others NEED without trying to guess what is troubling their souls. I start each day praying for my NEEDS often unknown as I face a new day. As I view the multitude of special college young people where I work making their way in a hurting complex world I pray constantly for their NEED.

We are commanded to come boldly to the "Throne of Grace" bringing our NEEDS and concerns. Therefore, each of us can follow the teaching to "PRAY WITHOUT CEASING" as we reach out to hundreds, even the vast unknown as we speak to OUR FATHER IN HEAVEN about the NEEDY in JESUS NAME!

OVERWHELMED!

Over the years I have learned one indisputable fact about the character of GOD and HIS attributes. They are revealed by His many defining names. **JEHOVAH-JIREH** means GOD WILL PROVIDE! I have collided with this aspect of HIS love and grace at special times of need. OVERWHELMED is the response of my heart every time. It is not only GOD's provision, but always at THE RIGHT TIME. Thus, all my angst and worry need never to have been.

I see Abraham's faith from the Old Testament Scripture where we read that he acted on GOD'S plan. He took Isaac his son to the mountain top to offer him as a sacrifice to God. Abraham told those men that went with him, WE WILL RETURN, revealing his trust in GOD'S plan! This whole event surely tested Abraham but revealed GOD'S love and grace. For at that moment Abraham raised the knife to offer his son, the ram in the bush was provided for the sacrifice, JEHOVAH-JIREH. The whole drama was about GOD'S PROVISION, NOT ABRAHAM'S PERFORMANCE.

This has proven so throughout my faith journey. The realities of GOD'S PROMISES AND HIS PROVISION always happen at the right time. At that moment I was always OVERWHELMED WITH AN UNSPEAKABLE JOY. I am still filled with unspeakable gratitude for those who served as conduits for sharing with me the privilege of knowing and serving the FATHER. I am thankful today for the watchfulness and faithfulness of JEHOVAH JIREH who spoke through those who shared with me.

I THANK GOD FOR HIS FAITHFULNESS. He reminds us to turn our heart toward Him daily, LISTENING BY THE SCRIPTURES thus ALLOWING THE HOLY SPIRIT TO EMPOWER US DAILY TO BEAR ONE ANOTHER'S BURDENS AND FULFILL THE LAW OF CHRIST, AS GOD SUPPLIES OUR EVERY NEED OUT OF HIS ABUNDANCE IN CHRIST JESUS! CHOOSING HIS PROVISION!

PATINA!

Patina is a coating or covering on anything that hides the real substance of the thing viewed. In the world of antiques, it can add value, but in the world of grace it must be removed to reveal the true nature of the subject. Thus, when you scratch the PATINA you discover what is underneath. Over the years I have encountered people who assumed the attitude of "how good me and mine are" based on how they viewed themselves. They had developed a certain PATINA that fit their image of themselves.

Scripture declares,

"As a man thinks so is he."

Once we choose a certain color or cover it becomes the PATINA we use to define ourselves. That becomes our measure of "realness" with our ACQUIRED way of thinking about ourselves as being "true." Thus, our PATINA locks us into a way of thinking that becomes what we wish to be, but not necessarily who we really are.

John Newton who gave us the song, Amazing Grace, wrote the following;

"The Lord leads me in the course of my preaching to insist much on a life of communion with Himself. By His

mercy nothing appears in my outward conduct (PATINA) to contradict what I say. Those who judge by what they see, suppose I live a very happy life. But alas, if they knew what passes in my heart, how dull my spirit is in secret, and how little I am myself affected by the glorious truths I propose to others, they would form a different judgement."

Newton dared to scratch his PATINA and reveal who he really was. Newton continues,

"PRAY for me, my dear friend, I am a poor, changeable, inconsistent creature; but God deals graciously with me, HE does not leave me wholly to myself. I have such daily proofs of the malignity of the sin that dwelleth in me, as ought to cover me with shame and confusion of face, making me thankful I am permitted to rank with the lowest who sit at His feet."

As new believers we tend to want to "act like a Christian" according to the standard set by those with whom we fellowship. It is then that we develop a PATINA that becomes our image. Sooner or later we realize that God's power operates best in our lives when we deal "RIGHT ON" with our brokenness and inability and His abounding LOVE and GRACE. It is then that we will forever surrender our "phony piety" and "performance self-righteousness," and ditch our developed PATINA, counting all things but dung for the excellence of the knowledge of JESUS CHRIST,

HIS DEATH, BURIAL AND RESURRECTION.

I have often said that if people knew me as God knows me, they would have nothing to do with me. THUS CHRIST IN US THE HOPE OF GLORY! CHOOSING GOD'S PROVISION RATHER THAN MY PERFORMANCE!

PLAYER / COACH

A COACH is one who instructs, a mentor, a tutor, one who brings truth from any discipline. He reveals an authority or truth and walks with you through it! The HOLY SPIRIT is the one who teaches believers and guides us into truth. The player/coach simply points a person to the Scriptures, introducing precepts and concepts of God's truth and instructing the one being coached to search the Scriptures asking questions and questioning answers.

I have often pondered why so few are discipled. Many declare salvation in Jesus Christ, many "join churches" and many attend meetings and listen to sermons, by way of tape, disc, TV, radio and personal attendance. Discipleship reveals itself by following Christ in a personal walk and relationship. Searching the Scriptures, seeking spiritual intimacy and experiencing power in the life of faith 24/7, is special.

Thus, those seeking answers for life's questions as well as questioning answers, canned or scripted, are few and far between. Each of us are at various levels in our walk and have a need to know what the Scriptures declare in their proper context and application. Over the years we have related to the idea of a pastor/people view of spiritual growth and development with the sermon as the primary instrument of challenge and teaching.

Some ministries use the idea of Sunday School, small groups or Bible classes to supplement the sermons. Most deal with life and its many issues by "calling the preacher." In this culture of spiritual apathy and skepticism we must address the lives of hurting people on a personal level. You go to a doctor, a lawyer or an accountant and demand a one to one relationship. In our spiritual growth we need someone in our face to personally address our walk and be accountable by dialogue not monologue.

Someone said that evangelism is "one beggar telling another beggar where the bread is." If that be the case then discipleship is sharing the bread, helping others who have found the bread of life know how to feed and pass on its nourishment to others. Jesus chose ordinary men to follow Him and be His disciples. Our greatest joy is sharing our journey with another so we both grow in grace and knowledge.

The player/coach concept of discipleship can be a part of EACH believer's lifestyle. The pastor/preacher position in this culture sometimes carries an air of academics and knowledge, thought unattainable by the ordinary believer. Player/coach is an understandable term that addresses the simplest soul. Every believer can immediately begin the player/coach relationship in his/her walk. The player is any believer having trusted Jesus Christ for the forgiveness of sin and begins searching the Scriptures. In sports a player is a participant, not a spectator. We have created a religious culture of spectators who GO "to church" stand, sit, sing, observe, listening to sermons or lectures rather than BE the church.

We as believers are all players having received the gift of God's love and grace referred to as salvation. We as individuals are the church. We gather and scatter as believers huddling for the purpose of "stimulating one another to love and good works" then back to the line of scrimmage for the daily "playing out" of the reality of GOD'S life in us. Our relationship to God is an individual relationship with Jesus Christ, a part of the corporate people of God worldwide. CHOICES MAKE A DIFFERENCE!

PAUL'S LEGACY!

Paul the Apostle authored powerful missionary letters. His legacy addresses us at three levels, his RESUME, his RULE and his RELEASE. Paul would never have made the grade in this world of trial sermons and how you look and perform. The Corinthians said of him, "not much to look at and couldn't speak very well." Paul's RESUME was "Chief of Sinners," "Least of the Apostles" and "A Nobody"! Paul was all about God's Provision not his performance. Paul's RULE was "Faith," "Freedom" and "Faithfulness"! On the BASIS OF FAITH was his rule of thumb for his "Jesus Walk" and all that he believed about the death, burial and resurrection of JESUS the author and finisher of his FAITH!

FREE from all men he chose to be a BOND SLAVE OF CHRIST and A SERVANT of all declaring that it was for FREEDOM we had been set FREE. His desire was to be found a FAITHFUL SERVANT to the end. Finally, his RELEASE was "Proclamation, Power and Presence." Paul RELEASED his personhood bound up IN CHRIST his "Hope of Glory" thus "to live was Christ and to die was gain." The Gospel was first and always the POWER of God unto salvation and in that truth his life was at one with God's POWER, period. Paul's final and ultimate reality was to be absent from the body and in the very PRESENCE of the LORD JESUS CHRIST!

This legacy was not just his but also for each believer who responds to the provision of the ABUNDANCE OF GOD'S GRACE, THE GIFT OF RIGHTEOUSNESS, ON THE BASIS OF FAITH! Our personal ministry to others is not about social standing, education, personality or talents but GOD'S GIFTING AND DESIRE FOR OUR LIFE. The call of God is personal and designed for us alone.

We are not a cookie cutter people who are all alike. As believers we are imperfect and broken but highly favored and forgiven, set apart and gifted for God's glory and mankind's redemption. This LEGACY OF PAUL is also ours provided BY GOD'S AMAZING GRACE ALONE and received BY FAITH ALONE! CHOOSE TO BE USED!

PONDERING!

In my early 20s I traveled as an evangelist, speaking at church, camps and city-wide youth crusades. Then I was employed by larger ministries as Minister of Youth. Later while serving as a pastor in Charlotte, NC of Wilmont Church the ministry to youth and children expanded. Beach trips, youth choirs, ball teams and the use of our gym for various ministries expanded our Gospel outreach. Eventually with the help of wonderful, serving people, the Agapé Center for drug counseling, support for addicted youth, the Community Food and Clothes Closet, Youth for Christ and the Charlotte Rescue Mission were exciting opportunities to share Jesus and the Gospel with our world.

Out of these efforts grew a kindergarten and day school. When we outgrew our facilities, these same wonderful dedicated people built Carolina Christian Day School, Kindergarten, Day Care and Fellowship, including Youth Ranch and an Institute of Biblical Studies. Those days were special and very busy.

My own spiritual journey was nurtured by older men and women who had a heart for the Lord and a love for me and my walk. The Scripture declares that older men and women should teach the younger. The following poem has been a reminder of what really matters. I have discovered in dealing with all ages MORE IS CAUGHT THAN TAUGHT!

> I took a piece of plastic clay
> And idly fashion it one day
> And as my fingers pressed it still
> It moulded, yielding to my will.
>
> I came again when days were past
> The bit of clay was firm at last
> The form I gave it still it wore
> And I could change that form no more.
>
> A far more precious thing than clay
> I gently shaped from day to day
> And moulded with my fumbling art
> A young child's soft and yielding heart.
>
> I watched that child as years did pass
> A full grown person was manifest
> With character set like harden clay
> So that none could change it any way.
>   -Lynetta Jones-

GOD ALONE CAN CHANGE THAT HARDENED CLAY, BUT BETTER TO BUILD A STRONG FOUNDATION FROM THE START. 'TIS LESS TO FORGET. CHOOSE TO SERVE!

TATER TIME!

In the world I grew up in the grand-maws used to tell us impatient, impulsive kids, JUST PEEL ONE TATER AT A TIME. Here are 4 potatoes that define who we might be at any given time as we confront our daily Faith Journey. One potato, two potato, three potato, four…etc., etc., and thus we counted people either in or out of a game with this little rap about potatoes. This blog uses a little "tongue in cheek" for reviewing life applications using the lowly POTATO!

POTATO #1 is a **SPEC-TATOR**, useless and given to viewing only what pleases him or herself. The spec-tator provides very little contribution to others, mostly self-gratification. We all have lived on this street one time or another, "…seeking our own way, not the way of the Lord." The spec-tator is more about talk and opinion than our walk.

POTATO #2 is the **COMMENT-TATOR**, with a comment on everything whether relevant or not. It often takes much time and misspeaking for any of us to be humbled into listening more and commenting less especially when all the facts are not available. I have been a member of this club far too often. When our comments are not based on truth or the facts, as the old timers used to say, "he just likes to hear himself talk" we end up misleading others.

The Scripture declares,

"...take no part in wrong and foolish talk, for those who do so will go farther into evil, (misleading others and deceiving ourselves)."

POTATO #3 is the **AGI-TATOR** who often has a chip on his or her shoulder, deep in insecurity or filled with anger about some unresolved situations. They are always stirring up do-do. Some personalities seem to live in this mode and are difficult to live with. There have been those times when all of us have been infected with this problem.

Scripture declares,

"...it is my desire, brothers, that you will take note of those who are causing division and trouble among you and keep away from them. For such people are not servants of the Lord, but of their pride; and by their smooth and well-said words, the hearts of those who have no knowledge of the truth, are tricked."

POTATO #4 is the **FACILI-TATOR** who in my humble opinion is the "sweet potato" and the best of all. He or she looks out for the interest of others to help them and encourage them to understand a given matter and to succeed. To me if "hot" means the best and the sharpest, then this tator is the "Hot Potato"! This potato "makes a difference" and is a blessing to others.

Scripture declares,

"Do nothing through envy or pride, but with humility, love others as you love yourself"! We daily CHOOSE which potato we will be!

POTHOLES!

Our Journey along life's highway is not always smooth but often finds us confronting unexpected POTHOLES. Those moments can distract and divert us from our Journey or become an occasion for learning and rethinking our lives and our Journey. God allows and uses such moments major or minor to draw us closer to Him. Too much smooth sailing leads us into a "look how good I am doing" arrogance. I have lived on that street and then hit an unexpected pothole or glitch. Those moments quickly magnify what is most important in our lives.

During the past two months I have lost several precious people in my life. Just recently at the passing of a dear friend I met a new beautiful family that would contribute unexpected blessings to the more mundane part of my daily life. Since the early eighties I have owned computers for writing and they have been a part of my Journey. My handwriting is a fright, and much too slow for my thinking and writing, and when it grows cold it is unreadable. I have had computer problems over the years, but a few weeks ago my primary writing machine crashed and was too costly for repair on my limited budget. It was a large pothole in my daily routine, but it refocused my Journey and became an unexpected blessing. I had prayed for direction, as a friend of my friend declared his experience with "computer repair." I was overwhelmed with the timing of my need and his statement. Answered prayer or coincidence? He took my much-needed computer and returned them working perfectly.

Having been without a working computer, God placed in my life just at the right time the right person and a new friend. The two weeks away from writing had given me some special time for thought and meditation. Also, I found that I missed my many old and new digital friends. Though we never see each other in the flesh we daily share digitally the joys and sorrows of one another's lives till we gather on the other side.

Man's technology can be either a blessing or a curse. What was a major frustration and a minor pothole in my daily Journey at that time became a major unexpected blessing. I can be sure there will be more major POTHOLES, including pain and hurt. BUT ONCE AGAIN I HAVE DISCOVERED THAT THE GOD OF THE SMOOTH ROAD IS ALSO THE GOD OF OUR POTHOLES NO MATTER HOW MINOR OR MAJOR THEY MAY BE!

PRAYER!

PRAY WITHOUT CEASING IS A COMMAND OF Scripture! I have come to the conclusion after many years of God adjusting my thinking and observing religious nonsense that it is more important to talk to God about people that to people about God.

We then trust God for the right word at the right time in speaking to people about God, as the Scriptures declares,

> *"BE READY TO GIVE A REASON OF THE HOPE WITHIN YOU TO THOSE WHO ASK."*

> *"PRAYING IN THE SPIRIT ACCORDING TO THE WILL OF GOD."*

Prayer is not a planned performance but an overflow of the believer's SPIRITUAL BREATHING. Trying to form prayers with words becomes an exercise in frustration.

Over the years I have participated in many group prayer circles where oral prayers were expected, as each person tried to manifest in words their burdens and concerns. Often one becomes more concerned about what others think of their piety instead of freely addressing the Father. Over the years my oral prayers have become briefer and without embellishment as if I had to remind the Father who I am and who He is in my life.

We are commanded to

"COME BOLDLY TO THE THRONE OF GRACE."

These days I awake remembering the words of David,

"MEDITATE IN YOUR HEART UPON YOUR BED AND BE STILL, BE GRACIOUS AND HEAR MY PRAYER, I RISE BEFORE DAWN AND CRY FOR HELP, I WAIT FOR YOUR WORD"!

"WE DO NOT KNOW HOW TO PRAY AS WE OUGHT,"

declares Scripture.

Prayer should indeed be WITHOUT CEASING, no mumbling or pious forms, just an honest direct appeal to ABBA FATHER / DADDY IN JESUS NAME. Jesus reminds us that prayer is not about many words and "vain repetitions"! Thus, daily WITHOUT CEASING is manifest three ways in our lives; the early WATCH, the early hours, the daily WAR, the struggle throughout the day, the evening WILT, tired and weary we wilt and rest in gratitude for another day.

It is always helpful to pray the Scriptures! Prayers consist daily of the cries for HELP in behalf of ourselves and others along with THANKSGIVING to the Father for HIS FAITHFULNESS FILLED WITH

MERCY, LOVE AND GRACE!

KING DAVID ILLUSTRATES HOW HE PRAYED TO GOD!

You are kind God! Please have pity on me. You are always merciful! Please wipe away my sins. Wash me clean from all my sin and guilt. I know about my sins, and I cannot forget my terrible guilt. You are really the one I have sinned against; I have disobeyed you and have done wrong. So, it is right and fair for you to correct and punish me. I have sinned and done wrong since the day I was born. But you want complete honesty, so teach me true wisdom. Wash me until I am clean and whiter than snow. Let me be happy and joyful! You crushed my bones, now let them celebrate. Turn your eyes from my sin and cover my guilt. Create pure thoughts in me and make me faithful again. Don't chase me away from you or take your Holy Spirit away from me. Make me as happy as you did when you saved me; make me want to obey! I will teach sinners your Law, and they will return to you. Keep me from any deadly sin. Only you can save me! Then I will shout and sing about your power to save. Help me to speak, and I will praise you, Lord. Offerings and sacrifices are not what you want. The way to please you is to know sorrow deep in our hearts. This is the kind of sacrifice you won't refuse.

THIS IS THE PRAYER OF KING DAVID AFTER HIS SINS OF ADULTERY, BETRAYAL AND MURDER. IT ALSO ADDRESSES MY HEART AS I DAILY SEEK

GOD'S FACE IN PRAYER AS I DEAL WITH MY SIN
AND BROKENNESS!

REBOUND

REBOUND is a word I remember from days of high school basketball. When a shot was missed or a play ended in a foul, coach would cry aloud, "REBOUND," meaning you messed up, but get back in the game, it is not over. Jesus reveals His amazing grace to Peter, the impetuous disciple who denied Him three times. In so doing we see GOD'S heart toward the inconsistent Peter who in moments of weakness failed.

The Scripture declares,

> *"...don't sin, but if you do you have an advocate with the Father, JESUS CHRIST the righteous."*

It was Peter when some disciples left Jesus that was asked by JESUS whether he would also leave. Peter answered, YOU HAVE THE WORDS OF LIFE THERE IS NO WHERE ELSE TO GO! JESUS confronted the disciples for their inability to stay awake when He went to pray. When Judas betrayed Jesus, Peter drew a sword and cut off the ear of a guard and was told to sheath his sword. JESUS also told Peter at one point that He was praying for him. It was later that Peter would deny Jesus three times, I DO NOT KNOW THIS MAN.

Jesus in in His third appearance for breakfast after the resurrection with the disciples, addressed Peter about his love for Him three times. Jesus used the UNCONDITIONAL word for love while Peter no doubt still hurting over his PUBLIC denial of JESUS, used the word for brotherly love, and was told to FEED HIS SHEEP. After the coming of the HOLY SPIRIT as promised by JESUS, Peter's powerful message to the multitude revealed the power of that UNCONDITIONAL LOVE. The final word of JESUS to Peter was how he would die, declaring "FOLLOW ME"! Peter would die a martyr.

The principle of REBOUND addresses Peter's brokenness and failures, yet Jesus continues reaching out to him as if he never sinned, thus JUSTIFICATION APPLIED.

THE SCRIPTURES declare,

> *"Therefore being JUSTIFIED (Just-if-ied never sinned) by FAITH, we have PEACE WITH GOD through our LORD JESUS CHRIST: by whom also we have access by FAITH into this GRACE wherein we STAND and rejoice in HOPE of the GLORY OF GOD."*

Thus, each of us as believers continually confront SPIRITUAL WARFARE and our temporary denials of GOD'S PROVISION. Our HUMAN PERFORMANCE fails and our sin is obvious, yet JESUS CHRIST, who died, was buried, and rose from the dead, revealing the GOOD NEWS of HIS ETERNAL LOVE AND GRACE, CRIES ALOUD by the HOLY SPIRIT and THE WORD, REBOUND! Thus, we as BELIEVERS CONFESS our SIN (our foul), REBOUNDING as if we never sinned.

ONLY GOD KNOWS THE HEART of EACH OF US, and HE alone KEEPS THE SCORE and TOTES THE NOTE. KEEP SHORT ACCOUNTS WITH GOD. LET YOUR LIFE BE A SALTY TREAT MAKING OTHERS THIRST FOR THE WATER OF LIFE. JUST A FEW GRAINS OF SALTY GRACE WILL BRING FLAVOR TO YOUR CONVERSATIONS AND ACTIONS. REMEMBER, TOO MUCH SALT CHOKES. MEASURE THE SALT OF GRACE WITH LOVE AND COMPASSION BUT BE SALT!

DARKNESS IS THE ABSENCE OF LIGHT HAVING ALSO ITS OWN REALITY. BE LIGHT BY BEING REAL IN YOUR WALK WITH THE LORD! BE SPIRITUAL IN NATURAL MATTERS AND NATURAL IN SPIRITUAL MATTERS. LIGHT IS QUIET AND IT MANIFESTS ITSELF IN CARING ATTITUDES AND SIMPLE ACTS OF KINDNESS, OPENING DOORS FOR YOUR LIGHT TO SHINE, SO BE LIGHT!

These truths remind me daily who I should be before

a needy, hurting broken world. I often miss the mark but REBOUND to be the SALT and LIGHT as GOD ENABLES ME.   CHOOSE DAILY TO REBOUND!

JESUS WHO?

JESUS A LUNATIC?

> *"...Jesus came home, and the crowd gathered again, to such an extent that they could not even eat a meal. When His own (kin) heard of this, they went out to take custody of Him; for they were saying, HE HAS LOST HIS SENSES."*

When humans choose to follow a fanatical man or woman, a lunatic, being drawn into their spell, by a strong emotional appeal, more TALK than WALK, they end up going down in flames. Was Jesus a lunatic?

JESUS A LIAR?

> *"...Jesus said it is My Father who glorifies Me, of whom you say, He is our God, and you have not come to KNOW Him, but I KNOW HIM; and if I say that I do not know Him, I will be a LIAR like you, but I do KNOW HIM and keep HIS WORD."*

JESUS constantly appealed to the TRUTH of who HE was. HE gave of HIMSELF, offering love and compassion to the most lowly and disposed of society.

JESUS A LEGEND?

> *"...The Jews were seeking JESUS at the feast and*

were saying, "Where is HE"? There was much grumbling among the crowds concerning HIM; some were saying, "He is a good man," "a good teacher;" others were saying, "No, on the contrary, He leads the people astray."

Legends appeal to our desire for human icons and a sense of knowing someone on center stage. We idolize the actor, performer, athlete, artist and even the preacher, often refusing to see their true character and believing that they really are just flesh and blood. The legend creates the idol, and the idol creates the legend. JESUS set the standard by living out the TRUTH HE proclaimed in the presence of ordinary people in everyday circumstances, manifesting HIS deity with love and grace. His followers saw it and responded. Was Jesus just a Legend?

JESUS THE LORD?

JESUS DECLARED,

"You do not want to go away do you"?

Peter answered,

"LORD TO WHOM SHALL WE GO? YOU HAVE THE WORDS OF ETERNAL LIFE. WE HAVE BELIEVED AND HAVE COME TO KNOW THAT YOU ARE THE HOLY ONE OF GOD."

JESUS declared HIMSELF to be the Way, the Truth

and the Life, the only way to the Father and then set out to manifest it by HIS LIFE, LOVE and GRACE. He was GOD in skin, dying for mankind's sin, our covering, as we TRUST HIM as our SAVIOR. As eternal LIGHT and LIFE, HE gives the gift "of HIS righteousness," revealing ABOUNDING GRACE in our behalf, FOR OUR SIN! Dying on the CROSS and then RESURRECTED. WE CHOOSE WHO HE IS TO US! LUNATIC, LIAR, LEGEND OR LORD! As believers we "…fix our eyes on JESUS, the author and perfecter of faith."

THESE THINGS HAVE BEEN WRITTEN SO THAT WE MAY BELIEVE THAT JESUS IS THE CHRIST, THE SON OF GOD; AND THAT BELIEVING WE HAVE LIFE IN HIS NAME. JUST GIVE ME JESUS! We each must CHOOSE!

SHEATH YOUR SWORD!

When Jesus was betrayed by Judas in the garden, Peter took a sword and sliced the ear off one of the soldiers who had come to arrest JESUS. Jesus immediately commanded, SHEATH YOUR SWORD! We live in a world of religious diversity and division. Religion is about man binding himself back to God or his gods by his good works. As a result, mankind has put their spin on who God is and how to approach Him and it is called religion.

Multitudes of faithful believers identify with small groups who love Jesus and His Word and are unaffiliated. There are cults and other religions who are commanded by strong personalities who create a following, emphasizing certain parts of the Bible or religious books while demanding that all believe without question. Some religions demand death to those who do not believe their system. The Scripture declares that Jesus came to seek and save the lost. His death, burial and resurrection reveal a relationship built on His work in our behalf, not our work, His righteousness, not ours.

Thus, as we confront those whose rituals and routines have been adjusted to their understanding and traditions we must with great humility share Jesus and the Word. Over the years hundreds of sects, denominations, religious forms and formulas have attached itself to Jesus, many declaring themselves as the ONLY WAY. Early in my walk with the Lord I thought it my responsibility to set matters right. I would draw my self-righteous SWORD to set things right with the sword of my understanding at that time. Over time I began understanding SHEATHING MY SWORD knowing that the Holy Spirit alone convicts the world of sin, righteousness and judgement. I can hear in my head Jesus saying, "SHEATH YOUR SWORD!"

The bottom line is not a Jesus religion but a Jesus relationship, with Him being the author and finisher of our faith. We have no ability nor right to judge the heart and soul of another and never considering ever to kill someone that refuses to believe God and receive His love and grace. We are to be a conduit of God's Love and grace even as we stand against corruption and evil. Love as a verb has muscle and courage, offering at the same time hope and forgiveness. History reveals men in the name of God doing dumb and violent things because of difference in understanding of God and His Word.

Though there are other religions which demand destroying those who do not accept their religious system.

The Bible declared that,

> *"we are not to wrangle about words to the ruin of the hearers."*

We must guard our own hearts and when people speak and declare their relationship to Jesus we must allow God alone to judge the intent of their hearts. The thief on the cross reminds us that people in the last moment of their lives may turn to God. That person may die in grace but miss that blessed journey of faith.

I must daily learn to SHEATH MY SWORD trusting God the Holy Spirit to honor His Word. Though we walk in the flesh our warfare is in God's just and merciful control not ours. Therefore "it is Christ in us the hope of glory" as we confront our world and it's many religious systems.

I PRAY THAT WE WILL HOLD UP JESUS, HIS DEATH, BURIAL AND RESURRECTION AND PROCLAIM, "LOOK AND LIVE," AS WE SHEATH OUR SWORDS AND STAND UPON GOD'S LOVE AND GRACE ALONE, TRUSTING THE SWORD OF THE SPIRIT, GOD'S ETERNAL WORD AND THE HOLY SPIRIT WITH THE FINAL WORD. I HEREBY WILL SHEATH MY SWORD TO GOD'S GLORY AND

MY GOOD!   A CHOICE!

BS EXCHANGED

A world of broken promises and lies has been attached to the letters BS. A redefining of those letters used to echo disappointment, hurt, pain, broken dreams, lies, betrayal, deceptions, schemes and a multitude of other religious untruths! Jesus confronted the BS'ers of His day who B-blindly S-suffocated the people with religious laws they themselves didn't keep. From a child I heard BS fall off the tongues of others even before I understood the anger life could bring to me, revealed by this simple verbal expression, while dealing with the unacceptable.

I now know its meaning and how well it defines a moment of expressed frustration. We often are confronted by lying politicians, preachers and teachers of error, self-appointed philosophers who distort the truth and ordinary folks who have been misled or believed a lie. THANK GOD THERE IS AN EXCHANGE for those POTENT LETTERS which often express our outrage either outwardly or inwardly.

At 16 my life was invaded by my B-Beloved S-savior. Not religion nor arrogant piety but a personal relationship with JESUS CHRIST! A wonderful exchange of an angry rebellious heart for B-blessed S-salvation, not bought or wrought but a gift of God's righteousness. As a believer dealing with the war within my old nature there is another BS exchange which empowers our life and feeds our inner man. The ultimate weapon for daily strength and wisdom in our life is B-bible S-study. This is a lifetime pursuit that daily changes our lives. Wisdom and strength comes by way of the SCRIPTURES and keeps us from failing and neglect, keeps us growing in grace.

My first speech teacher in college was "old school" and she demanded when I made speeches in class that I not use notes.

> *"Mr. Griffin when you speak never use notes but be filled with your subject so as to speak out of the overflow, looking into the eyes of your hearers,"*

truly B-believer S-speak.

Thus, our preparation to speak to others is to prepare ourselves by our daily walk and study of the Word. Out of the overflow of the mind and heart we will be B-battle S-strong and prepared to stand and give a reason of the hope within us.

Finally, each believer is under command to share God's grace becoming a B-blessed S-sower of God's Word as His B-bond S-servant.

THE MIRACLE OF GRACE IS AVAILABLE TO ALL HAVING TRANSFORMED US AS BELIEVERS BY THE DEATH, BURIAL AND RESURRECTION OF JESUS CHRIST. He has EMPOWERED US as B-burden S-sharers IN A BROKEN HURTING WORLD,

DAILY CHOOSING TO LIGHT A CANDLE RATHER THAN CURSING THE DARK. AMAZING GRACE HOW SWEET THE SOUND! RIGHT CHOICE!

REMEMBERING

Mordecai Ham impacted my life when I was a seminary student in Louisville, Kentucky. It was months before his death and we met at a church revival and became friends. I would spend personal time with him, taking him places and reviewing his past ministry. This led to friendship with his nephew, a writer and a recorder of many of Mordecai's endeavors. He gave me books of Mordecai's sermons and his biography. Mordecai detailed the gospel meeting in Charlotte, NC when Billy Graham, the Wilson boys, and others became believers.

I still cherish those moments of sharing with a man who God used to impact a community and a people for eternity! The seed Mordecai Ham sowed continues to bear eternal fruit thru the children of that Gospel meeting which was the answer to the praying of Billy's father and many others.

The work of Franklin Graham, other siblings, the children and grandchildren of Billy are putting shoes and a voice on the Gospel around the world. Billy gave the Word of God, the Gospel of JESUS CHRIST a mighty voice, which has produced children of faith for generations to come. Indeed, the faithfulness of Mordecai Ham in Charlotte years ago produced a harvest that keeps on growing and giving for eternity. BLESSED CHOICES!

GOD'S "HEY-BOY"

"What shall we do, that we may work the works of GOD"?

JESUS answered and said to them,

"This is the work of GOD that you believe in HIM whom GOD has sent."

"...the greatest among you shall be your SERVANT "HEY-BOY."

Time moves forward ever so quickly and represents new opportunities. Perhaps even new ways of seeing and applying what we know and who we are in this world. It is God alone who never changes as He is revealed in His Son, who is "the same yesterday, today and forever."

I have heard the term HEY-BOY all my life used in an off-the-cuff manner when defining a response to someone's need or command. In my spiritual journey I can remember how many "chore driven" things I was asked to do and I was reminded of the Scripture which commanded,

"Do all things without grumbling or disputing."

That was tough for me in those early days of my "faith walk" and there are even times now when it seems easier to grumble than to serve or be obedient.

Paul's constant declaration about being a

"bondservant" of Jesus Christ was interesting to me but a reminder that I hadn't gotten there yet. Inside religious systems that I often served, I was a "religious HEY-BOY," fulfilling others expectations. Thus, I did not approach my service with a joyful spirit but was driven by others who devised things for me to do. Commands that often made me a religious surrogate, that served neither God nor man with a proper attitude. I thank God those days are over for the most part. I have learned to define commands and expectations given by others by searching God's Word for my "place in the Son." I truly find great joy in being a HEY-BOY for the Father as it is played out in truly helping others and bearing their burdens.

I cannot truly help a person that will not help themselves. Thus, it is a joy to help others help themselves. I find when I connect with others and reach out to affirm and love them that I am strengthened and renewed. Learning to discern each person and their situation provides a blessing. The ability to say no to people at times and love them while refusing to be a part of their rebellion or self-righteousness, has been an exercise in growth. Grace, as does love, has a tough side that sets us free to be real, not posturing or pretending.

I love the Apostle Paul's exhalation so very much "...THOUGH I AM FREE FROM ALL MANKIND, I HAVE MADE MYSELF A SLAVE / A SERVANT, A HEY-BOY TO ALL, SO THAT I MAY WIN MORE." We each must pray daily that as HEY-BOYS we will know when to reach out and when to draw back, for both are essential to serving and loving properly. Only the Holy Spirit can be our guide as we press on in our walk with the Father.

We must never judge ourselves by others but REST in HIM and HIS guidance in our lives, always knowing that each of us who know Him on the "basis of faith" has a history of His way with us, FOR HIS GLORY AND OUR GOOD. Our over anxious flesh often thwarts God's doing a great work in and through us. We often have plans and energy, attempting to "get it done" for the Lord when we fall short and fail because it was more of us than Him. I have been there many times and each time I think, "I should have RESTED more IN HIM"!

IT IS NOT OUR JOB TO "GET IT DONE" BUT RATHER TO ALLOW HIM TO GET IT DONE IN HIS TIME, IN HIS WAY TO HIS GLORY AND OUR GOOD AS WE REST IN HIM WITH PATIENCE AND HUMILITY ALLOWING HIM TO USE US AS HE WILLS AS A CONDUIT OF HIS LOVE AND GRACE IN A HURTING WORLD!

GOT-IT-DONE!

We live in a world of "GIT-ER-DONE" made popular worldwide by a well-known comedian! This idiom has become a part of our culture and I too find it rolling easily off my tongue. Somehow when requesting someone to do something, it adds a touch of humor to the request. Religion has always emphasized the "DO and DON'T DO" factor which could be referred to as DO-DO! The outcome is the assumption that the more good you DO the better "your score" with God and others. In reality this is not so inside the spiritual brokenness and lostness of mankind.

The message of the gospel of Jesus Christ is not at all about mankind's PERFORMANCE but God's PROVISION.

> "...all the king's horses and all the king's men couldn't put Humpty Dumpty together again,"

after he fell off the wall breaking to pieces, so goes the nursery rhyme. All the most religious of men can't put the broken pieces of the "humpty dumpty" of our lives together. All the best religion effort and human PERFORMANCE cannot redeem mankind as it defiantly, and self-righteously declares with arrogance, watch us "GIT-ER-DONE"!

Before the foundation of the world God ordained that the redemption of mankind would be from HIS MIND TO OURS! The plan would be Salvation History progressed from the CREATION / THE FALL / SEED OF WOMAN / COVENANT / ISRAEL / MESSIAH / LORD JESUS CHRIST / HIS DEATH BURIAL AND RESURRECTION / HUMANITY UNTARNISHED – DEITY UNDIMINISHED! From the cruel Roman cross Jesus would declare the words that would echo from eternity to eternity, IT IS FINISHED to HE IS NOT HERE, HE IS RISEN thus HIS PROVISION.

In today's idiom it could sound like this, GOT-ER-DONE! Our salvation is the ABUNDANCE OF GOD'S GRACE, THE GIFT HIS RIGHTEOUSNESS! Thus religion, philosophy and psychology must now and forever surrender the impotent GIT-ER-DONE for the perfect work of our Lord and Savior Jesus Christ in our behalf. He GOT-ER-DONE! By Grace we are salvaged by Faith, not of ourselves, a gift not based on human PERFORMANCE but God's PROVISION! AMAZING GRACE HOW SWEET THE SOUND THAT SAVED A WRETCH LIKE ME! NEVER DO-DO BUT DONE!

GRATITUDE ATTITUDE!

"Grace to you and peace from God our Father and the Lord Jesus Christ. I THANK my God always, making mention of you all in my prayers…"

"Continue steadfastly in prayer, watching therein with THANKSGIVING;"

"…in everything give THANKS: for this is the will of God in Christ Jesus to you-ward."

"You are my God, and I will give THANKS to you: You are my God, I will exalt You. Oh, give thanks to the Lord; for He is good; For His loving-kindness endures forever."

Our greatest weapon against our old nature and the power of evil is an attitude of thanksgiving and gratitude expressed in our prayers and face to face with others.

Thanksgiving to God for His love, grace and forgiveness and to others who have made a difference in our life is primary. A twin of gratitude is generosity which enables us to be a giver rather than a taker. But it all starts with a thankful heart. We all have dysfunction in our lives from kin to personal brokenness and inability. Jesus declared that the "well needs no doctor." Thus our sufficiency is from God alone.

As we are chemically driven by hormones and moods, we confront daily a self-oriented world where it is easy to be overcome by self-righteousness, living by our feelings, comparing ourselves with others. Therefore, expectations create certain failure and negativity and quench a thankful heart. Once I discovered that I was my greatest enemy, I agreed with Scripture,

> *"Do not trust in mankind, and do not lean on your own understanding"*!

That is easy to say, but more difficult to apply living in my skin. God has seen fit to put many wonderful, imperfect, steadfast and focused people in my life who over the years have walked with me and loved me in spite of my warts. Thus, in turn I praise God for His love and grace and pray for the needs of others with THANKSGIVING. Even when names and faces elude me I recall moments when certain situations changed my way of thinking forever.

I grew up in a world where people dropped in and visited one another without appointment, sharing their lives and burdens. Sharing each other's burdens and communicating love by voice and text has become the order of the day. I have discovered the word "precious" these days for family, friends and their concerns, not because of my great sensitivity, but because of a greater value on the brevity of life, God's grace, and human suffering. When I hurt and struggle it is best alleviated by reaching out to others, loving and caring for their pain and need.

Perhaps this is what Scripture means when it declares:

"BEAR ONE ANOTHER'S BURDEN AND THUS FULFILL THE LAW OF CHRIST"!

Tell someone today that you LOVE them, and they are PRECIOUS with THANKSGIVING. A choice!

GROW UP!

The new believer is akin the human baby with a need for intimacy and nurture. We refer to spiritual child-raising as discipleship. A talking head and a faceless crowd cannot possibly nurture and mature a human baby or a new born believer in Jesus Christ. As a child I often heard a parent address a child with "grow up."

Growing in grace demands far more than sermons and lectures commanding us to 'grow up" often using guilt for correction. Spiritual intimacy will never happen without personal "in your face," "hands on" daily involvement "one to one." Thus, every baby believer must be parented, discipled by a faithful older believer, not a necessity to be the same biological age. As with the human child such caring is inconvenient and demanding but blessed. The feeding of the milk and the meat of God's Word calls for daily monitoring. Potty training of the baby believer is a way of expelling and voiding old patterns of thought and behavior from his or her way of life prior to their spiritual birth.

Growing up as a believer is a daily war with the old nature and the world order. Every believer must have instructions from the Word and constant guidance to grow through spiritual childhood into maturity. The Scriptures declare that older men and women must teach the younger! It is not easy to be an effective parent or a true disciple. It demands being inconvenienced and often living outside your comfort zone, yet a constant source of great joy and satisfaction. Again, Scripture reminds us that we are to "bear one another's burdens and fulfill the law of Christ."

The command to "GROW UP" IS FROM THE MIND OF God AND HIS WORD. Therefore, it is essential for each of us to grow in GRACE AND KNOWLEDGE TO GOD'S GLORY AND OUR GOOD. Search out an older believer and make them a prayer partner and mentor as you walk together in the Word and both of you will GROW. Remember Jesus sent His disciples out two by two. ACCOUNTABILITY A CHOICE!

POWER OF ONE!

The POWER OF ONE is our relationship to God and man, a personal relationship not a corporate enterprise.

Each believer is commanded to,

> *"Bear one another's burdens"*

as the HOLY SPIRIT empowers US to become light and salt in our daily world.

The measure of salt is not the beauty of the salt shaker but the power of each grain bringing GRACE'S flavor to all we encounter. Light is not about the light fixtures but the light of GOD'S LOVE AND GRACE through US in a dark world.

We gather for fellowship, encouragement, accountability and STUDYING GOD'S WORD. A Holy Huddle, then back to the line of scrimmage. We each have a witness empowered by the Holy Spirit who prepares individuals to receive the message of the GOOD NEWS, of Christ's death, burial and resurrection. We become a part of God's redemptive process as ONE TO ANOTHER, through prayer, a personal word or a work of grace, but it is always GOD who gives the increase, or result. God honors His empowering, impregnating Word. "FAITH comes by hearing and hearing by the WORD OF GOD," period.

We surrender our ONE to GOD not manipulating people with guilt and fleshly approaches of persuasion and salesmanship, producing a religion of do and don't do instead of "Amazing Grace' produced by the "done" and completed work of Christ's shed blood, His burial and resurrection. We have a great opportunity to affect the lives of those around us daily. Our "Power of One" depends on us being clothed with humility and a sense of God's righteousness not our own. Authenticity means that we stand in an authority greater than ours, not given to argument and debate, not "wrangling over words to the ruin of the hearers." Every person is obedient to some reality in their life, even if their obedience is to their own skewed self-centered values.

Obedience to God's authority in our lives is the only real source of meaning and joy. The natural man structures his/her life around themselves, their pleasures and their desires. Thus, there is a power of evil which one can spread and increase its influence by deceit and corruption. The power of OUR ONE flows from OUR INNER MAN founded on God's love and grace. Thus, daily WE deal with "flesh and Spirit" as we interact with each other and Scripture truth, until the day we depart our bodies. We, as JESUS, will have to pay the price for our stand as HE did. HE WAS ACCUSED OF BEING: AN ILLEGITIMATE CHILD, A DRUNKARD, A GLUTTON, A FALSE PROPHET, A DECEIVER, A BLASPHEMER, BEING MENTALLY ILL, DEMON POSSESSED, A LAW

BREAKER, AND SATAN INCARNATE. We can expect BEING MISUNDERSTOOD as we manifest "CHRIST IN US THE HOPE OF GLORY" AS SALT AND LIGHT.

HEART TO HEART!

The Scriptures have much to say about the HEART; not the blood pump but the core of our being. The Heart is declared deceitful, sick and wicked. Our first response might be disgust but when we observe the brokenness of relationships, inhumanity, violence and sexual excesses, we admit something is broken. A card, a promise, flowers and candy cannot fix it. The Scriptures speak of believers as trophies of Grace, a letter written on the HEARTS that all might see. We are encouraged to love God with all our HEARTS as He first loved us. Thus it is declared,

> *"HEREIN IS LOVE NOT THAT WE LOVE GOD BUT HE LOVES US."*

Jesus said to His disciples at the last supper,

> *"LOVE ONE ANOTHER AND BY THAT ALL WILL KNOW THAT WE ARE HIS DISCIPLES."*

FOR GOD SO LOVED THE WORLD HE GAVE US HIS ONE OF A KIND SON TO DIE ON A CROSS, BURIED AND RAISED FROM THE DEAD FOR OUR SIN DEBT. God's love is UNCONDITIONAL while mankind's love is very CONDITIONAL and many faceted. Human love is best spelled out as follows:

L *LOVE* – communion – spirit – communication - feelings - senses – FRIENDSHIP

I *INTIMACY* – prayer – humility – honesty - humor –

pleasure – hormones – RELATIONSHIP

K *KNOWLEDGE* – faithfulness – focus – spirituality - encouragement – loyalty – fulfillment – LORDSHIP

E *ENERGY* – change – endurance – sexuality – caring- flexibility – compromise – FELLOWSHIP

Love symbolized as a HEART is best expressed as LIKE. Human LOVE is manifest in many ways, but the marriage bond demands the strongest of commitments and growth. Thus, HEART TO HEART IS THE POWER OF SHARED HUMAN LOVE OVER THE YEARS IN MANY WAYS AND IS BEST EXPRESSED IN "I LIKE YOU" AND "YOU ARE MY FRIEND."

THEREFORE MUCH LOVE TO ALL MY FACEBOOK FRIENDS AS WE GROW IN GRACE AND REACH OUT TO ONE ANOTHER DIGITALLY IN THESE TROUBLED TIMES "HEART TO HEART." CHOICES OF THE HEART!

HERE I STAND!

HERE I STAND!

> *"IN GOD I HAVE PUT MY TRUST, I SHALL NOT BE AFRAID. WHAT CAN MAN DO TO ME?"*

I grew up all my life around "church," that is the organized, categorized, "only one got the real truth" church. As a pastor's kid I was exposed early to shrewd, manipulative people with agendas who affected my father and our family. I would often hear my father in quiet tones speak to my mother of the POLITICS in the church. Whether in the church or the government POLITICS can be a mean, vindictive, corrupting process that uses people as pawns and money as the trump card by which to control those who are "weak sheep."

We are living in a changing world and a changing culture here in America. We will never return to the past and if the truth be known, it too was equally as corrupt and difficult for its time. In the days of Scripture men lived under cruel dictatorships, and sometimes a benevolent king or ruler, but for the most part corrupt and controlling men, whose pride and arrogance dominated their domain. The word "POLITIC" is rooted in the word for 'citizen," the very people who are usually the receivers of corrupt and deceitful practices. Where must we stand as "believers" and followers of Jesus Christ and His Way? The SCRIPTURES tell us simply where to plant our feet and rest our minds and hearts. READ AND PRAY!

1. RENDER TO CAESAR WHAT IS CAESAR'S AND TO GOD WHAT IS HIS. JESUS
2. WE ARE TO PRAY FOR THOSE IN AUTHORITY WHETHER THEY BE GOOD OR BAD RULERS OVER US.
3. WE ARE NOT TO PUT CONFIDENCE IN MAN, BUT GOD
4. WE ARE NOT TO PUT CONFIDENCE IN GOVERNMENT, BUT GOD.
5. GOVERNMENT WHETHER GOOD OR BAD IS FOR OUR GOOD. THOUGH WE MAY NOT AGREE OR APPROVE OF IT AND ITS LEADERSHIP, IT GIVES SOME STRUCTURE AND PROTECTION TO OUR HUMAN EXISTENCE.
6. WE SHOULD SEEK TO LIVE A QUIET LIFE, MIND OUR OWN BUSINESS AND WORK WITH OUR OWN HANDS TO GOD'S GLORY AND OUR GOOD.
7. IN OUR FORM OF GOVERNMENT WE STILL ARE GIVEN THE OPTION OF APPEAL, VOTING OUR CONVICTIONS AND MAKING THEM KNOWN.

8. FINALLY, WE SHOULD SEEK TO BE GOOD CITIZENS BY OBEYING THE LAWS OF OUR LAND, STAYING OUT OF TROUBLE AS MUCH AS POSSIBLE. WE SHOULD PAY OUR BILLS AND SEEK TO HELP THE NEEDY AND HURTING AS OPPORTUNITY PROVIDES, SUFFERING FOR RIGHTEOUSNESS SAKE WHEN IT IS THRUST UPON US, AND NOT AS EVIL DOERS.

9. PRAYING WITHOUT CEASING FOR OUR COUNTRY, OUR WORLD AND ALL WHO GOVERN AND LEAD, AND FOR FREEDOM AND OPPORTUNITY FOR ALL MANKIND TO COME TO THE TRUTH OF GOD'S LOVE AND GRACE.

10. LOOKING UNTO JESUS THE AUTHOR AND FINISHER OF OUR FAITH.

11. *"But we have forgotten God. We have forgotten the gracious Hand which preserved us in peace, and multiplied and enriched and strengthened us; and we have vainly imagined, in the deceitfulness of our hearts…"*

President Abraham Lincoln

"STAND FIRM THEREFORE, having girded your loins with truth and having put on the breast-plate of righteousness… HERE I STAND, I cannot do otherwise, God help me. Amen."

Martin Luther

"We have rebelled against God. My brethren, let us repent and implore the divine mercy. May the Lord hear us in the day of trouble…We will rejoice in His salvation and in the name of our God, we will set up our banners"!

Samuel Langdon
President of Harvard University
May 1775 addressing the Provincial Congress of Massachusetts

I had a wedding at Harvard University in the historic chapel in the seventies and saw written on one of the buildings "For Christ and the Church." The founders of Harvard believed that "All Knowledge without Christ was vain." Not so today!

As Charles Dickens said,

"We live in the best of times and in the worst of times."

This statement though paraphrased is true. We are a blessed nation and we have been a blessing to the whole world. Yet, we live in troubled times. We as believers must find a balance between the extremes of religious, political and cultural extremes.

Our nation today is suffering because political agendas have captured minds that are more interested in getting than giving. It has nothing to do with right-wing or left-wing but a failure in our spiritual lives of being guided by GOD'S WORD, and in our political lives we have abandoned our CONSTITUTION and the RULE OF LAW for self-serving gain driven by money and power, rather than humility and service. We all must STAND OUR GROUND and look to God and His grace as individuals in our daily walk, realizing how sinful and broken we all are without the gift of God's righteousness.

HERO

The word HERO means different things to different people. I use it in relationship to ordinary people who put God's love and grace into shoe leather in this broken world. Thus bringing into our lives a spiritual nobility empowered by the Holy Spirit making a difference.

There are many among us whose deeds of kindness and quiet faithful service are by this standard HEROIC to God's glory and our good. The Scripture commands us to

> *"maintain good works for they are profitable unto men."*

Therefore, others

> *"see our good works and glorify the Father which is in heaven."*

May we as believers dare to be HEROIC in our faith walk in these troubled times. Then our identity in Christ will be declared more by who we are and how we live than a list of Do and Don't Do!

WORK OF GOD!

"This is the work of GOD that you believe in Him whom GOD has sent."

"...the greatest among you shall be your SERVANT"

JESUS

TIS IMPORTANT TO RENEW DAILY OUR VISION OF THE NATURE AND CHARACTER OF God and who we are because of who He is. Time moves forward ever so quickly and presents new opportunities and ways of seeing and applying what we know and who we are in the world.

In my spiritual journey I remember how "chore driven" I have been at times and am reminded of the Scripture which commands,

"Do all things without grumbling or disputing."

That was tough for me in those early days of my "faith walk" and there are even times now when it seems easier to grumble than to serve others. Paul's constant declaration about being a "bondservant" of Jesus Christ was interesting to me, but a reminder that I had more growing to do.

I have discovered that so many of the "churchy" religious things attached to my walk with the Lord were not commands from the FATHER but institutional obligations that never contributed to my growing in grace. Inside church systems that I often served, I was a "religious HEY-BOY," fulfilling expectations. Thus I did not approach my service with a joyful spirit, but was driven by others who devised things for me to do and commands to fulfill that often made me a religious surrogate. Therefore, I neither served God or man with a proper attitude. I thank God those days are over for the most part.

I have learned to define commands given by others and expectations that are not acceptable, and search God's Word for my "place in the Son." I have also realized that I cannot help a person that will not help themselves. It is rewarding to help others help themselves. I now find when I am dealing with my own inabilities and frustrations that reaching out to others renews my walk and my priorities. The ability to say "no" to people at times, refusing to be a part of their rebellion or self-righteousness, calls for wisdom and understanding.

Grace, as does love, has a tough side that sets us free to be real, without posturing or pretending. ...THOUGH I AM FREE FROM ALL MANKIND, I HAVE MADE MYSELF A SLAVE / A SERVANT, A HEY-BOY TO ALL, SO THAT I MAY WIN MORE.

APOSTLE PAUL   As SPIRITUAL HEY-BOYS we learn when to reach out and when to draw back, for both are essential to serving and loving properly. The bottom line is the more of a servant we become the more we mature in the Lord, desiring to be the FATHER'S HEY-BOY making the most of opportunities to serve others, that our joy be full. The secret to such service is learning that we don't work for GOD, but the FATHER works in and through us to do His good pleasure, as we walk in HIS way.

IT IS NOT OUR JOB TO "GET 'ER DONE," BUT RATHER TO ALLOW HIM TO GET IT DONE IN HIS TIME, IN HIS WAY, TO HIS GLORY AND OUR GOOD AS WE REST IN HIM WITH PATIENCE AND HUMILITY ALLOWING HIM TO USE US AS HE WILLS AS CONDUITS OF HIS LOVE AND GRACE. BE A CARING HEY-BOY IN A BROKEN, HURTING WORLD BEARING ONE ANOTHER'S BURDENS, FULFILLING THE LAW OF CHRIST.   A CHOICE!

HOLY SELFIE

Life is good and very busy, God is gracious! I am blessed, daily needing time to take stock of my walk with the Lord. Looking at my character, convictions, compromises and inconsistencies! My warts and brokenness are obvious to me therefore I need time for a spiritual "DEFRAGMENTATION."

Painful at first, for sin of any kind is unacceptable, demanding confession, repentance, a renewing of the mind and Spirit. Then comes the power of God's grace and forgiveness with the unspeakable joy of an honest confession of inability. Transgressions and iniquities rob one's victories. All these vestiges of sin revealed by the Light of God's Word restore the soul and in moments of quietness allow us to hear the sweet voice of the Holy Spirit. There is nothing like a hot bath when the grime of living in the fast lane clogs one's pores.

I thank God for compassionate, caring believers who love me unconditionally as we pray for one another. The treasure of God's grace indwells the "clay pot" of our flesh, helping us realize that the glory is God's not ours. Therefore, may we daily determine to find time in our "busy world" to seek out a quiet place, for taking a spiritual "inventory!" A "HOLY SELFIE" indeed!

LIFESTYLE FAITH!

"WHATSOEVER YOU DO, in WORD or in DEED, DO ALL in the name of the Lord Jesus, giving thanks to God the Father through JESUS,"

so speaks the Scripture.

We live in a world of diverse lifestyles, occupations and demands. Man, by nature is competitive desiring to win a game, an argument, a position or being better than his or her peers.

We grow up being compared to others, by parents, friends and ourselves. As believers in this highly diverse technically advanced world we may be involved in many occupations from all levels of the economic scale. Our gifts, talents, education level, physical skills and spiritual sensitivity cause us to occupy a particular place in our world. Thus, no matter our place, we are to do it all in Jesus name and to His glory in order to live our lives and make a difference for God's glory and our good. In all that we do, either passive or active we need to filter what it means in our relationship to our walk with the Lord and how it affects others.

Scripture declares that

"I am free from you all, but choose to be your servant."

Therefore, every occupation and vocation known to mankind reveals those who believe and trust Jesus Christ in a personal relationship. The real issue in the life of all believers is what one allows in his or her lifestyle in how we speak and what we take in with our mind and eye-gate. This requires learning to filter what comes into our mind and what goes out from the same.

We are not legalists as those in Christ are free to be all God can make us and we are commanded to judge our own behavior and not to stand in judgment of others. As believers we each must confront our lifestyle and how we walk out our faith and apply the Scriptures to our individual journey. We all are damaged and broken with treasures of God's grace dwelling in clay pots to the glory to God and not ourselves.

Jesus declared that the

> *"well need not a doctor"*

and that

> *"He came to seek and to save the lost"*

finding us while we were "broken."

We each one must work out the salvation that God

has given us, for He is in us to will and to do. Therefore, there is no place in a believer's life for FALSE PIETY AND SELF RIGHTEOUSNESS.

AVAILABILITY

We all have times of loneliness and hurt. Many have lost a loved one, confronted broken dreams, lost jobs or experienced disillusionment in life. A person wrapped up in himself makes a very small package. Life at best is filled with the unpredictable and the unexpected. Such matters bring a measure of hurt and pain.

The first response to such a change in our routine often is to retreat within ourselves, not revealing our emotional crisis, keeping our pride intact. We soon learn that this behavior only compounds our hurt and loneliness. I thank God for those whose concern for my wellbeing, dared to confront and invade my space over the years, being available.

Paul the former lawyer, bounty hunter, and finally a believer spoke of "conflicts without and fears within." Then, "came Titus" a friend whose very appearance brought comfort and encouraged Paul. Thus, when one moves outside themselves into another's space to give not take, the blessings run both ways. It enlarges our capacity for reaching out, deepens our burden for others and their need, diminishing our selfishness and strengthening another's.

Scripture declares,

"Bear one another's burdens and fulfill the law of Christ."

Our greatest joy as a believer is reaching out to others by being available. Every season of life brings with it an opportunity to reach out to the hurting and needy. Make a phone call, speak an encouraging word, or do a kind deed in someone's behalf. Such caring WILL MAKE A DIFFERENCE AS ONLY SMALL ACTS OF KINDNESS CAN! Perhaps we will CHOOSE to make AVAILABILITY a lifestyle.

DADDY! I HURT!

"...when the fullness of the time came, God sent forth His Son, born of a woman, born under the Law, so that He might redeem those who were under the Law, that we might receive the adoption of sons. Because you are sons, God has sent forth the Spirit of His Son into our hearts, crying, "ABBA! FATHER!* (DADDY)

* (The word "abba! Father!" is an Aramaic word of endearment and may be translated daddy)

JESUS CHRIST WAS BORN IN POVERTY, DIED IN PAIN, AGONY AND DISGRACE. HE HURT AND DIED FOR US, LOVE'S FREE GIFT! So much of my spiritual growth has come through the struggle with bad CHOICES, missed opportunities, confused thinking, thoughtlessness, selfishness, and my old sin nature. Philip Yancey in his wonderful book, "WHERE IS GOD WHEN IT HURTS" has listed some things that reveal positive realities to suffering, which involves hurt and pain:

- Suffering is the great equalizer, common to all.

- Suffering produces a dependence on God and those that are healthy, and interdependence on one another.

- Suffering causes us not to find our security in things that may soon be taken away.

- Suffering humbles the proud.

- Suffering causes cooperation not competition.

- Suffering helps distinguish necessities from luxuries.

- Suffering teaches patience born of dependence.

- Suffering helps us distinguish valid fears from exaggerated fears.

- Suffering people hear the Gospel as good news not as a threat or scolding.

- Suffering people can respond to the call of the Gospel with abandonment because they have so little to lose.

- Suffering gets our attention and causes us to listen with our inner ears, addresses our inner man.

- Suffering or affliction as it is often called in the Scriptures, gives us the ability to help others in their affliction.

When a father has to deal with the hurt and pain of

his small child he often hears the cry, "DADDY! IT HURTS!" and instantly sees the remedy for the pain. It touches our heart to hear a hurt child cry out in pain. As believers we know that God is indeed touched by our infirmities.

The Scriptures deal with the nature and character of God, who loves and cares for mankind. God chose a tribal people called Israel and through one man, Abraham, with whom He cut a covenant, a promise. The drama of salvation history is revealed in the Bible so that we can understand the heart of God and His desire for all of creation. The journey from Adam and Eve, to Noah, to Abraham, to Moses, to David and eventually Jesus Christ is filled with faith and failure, PAIN and HURT that God uses to His glory and the good of mankind.

Joseph said to his brothers,

> *"you meant evil against me, but God meant it for good."*

Thus situations, difficulties and failures at a moment in time may create hurt, pain and suffering, but eventually produce blessing and spiritual growth.

Scriptures declare that

> *"GOD CAUSES ALL THINGS TO WORK TOGETHER FOR GOOD TO THOSE WHO LOVE GOD, TO THOSE*

WHO ARE CALLED ACCORDING TO HIS PURPOSE."

Though HURT and PAIN is never pleasant, it produces in us spiritual and emotional growth. Sin in the life of the believer also brings PAIN and HURT; but with confession, fellowship and joy is restored. David's prayer of confession was out of his pain and hurt because of his sin. DADDY! I HURT! is a look at HURT as it is spelled out and how it's reality impacts our lives and how we come to experience it in our lives.

Hardship is manifest daily in various ways, whether in getting up, getting to work, school, appointed rounds, family matters or relationship problems. Our frame of mind, our chemistry or our circumstances greatly affect our measure of hardship that causes PAIN, and bring HURT to mind, body or feelings. We are really fragile and easily broken. Only God's wonderful grace, peace and love can sustain us. We are often our own greatest enemy. We as believers will also realize rejection in various ways, but God will always be our strength and wisdom. In some parts of the world today people are not only ridiculed but beaten and disowned. To be rejected because of our stupidity or foolishness is one thing, but to be rejected because of manifesting God's love and grace in our lives, is a matter that we must trust to the Father, as we suffer ridicule or rejection to His glory.

God's strength will become our strength as we cry out to Him, DADDY! I HURT! He will reply every time, "My Grace Is Sufficient"! We live in troubled times filled with conflict, wars, anger, violence, crudeness and unbelief bringing with it doubt about the future. With all our modern technology we find ourselves busied and burdened with cares and a culture that is totally materialistic. We often love things and use people instead of using things and loving people. Thus losing connection with intimacy and caring, rushing to and fro, becoming tired and weary. Past memories, failures, empty materialism, and spiritual lostness can make our daily lives more complicated. Only a true believer will understand this blog as it deals with God's provisions in our behalf.

Men and women love us then just as quick reject us because at some level we do not meet their expectation. My greatest hurt and rejection has often been more from my brother and sister in Christ than those estranged from God. We all often become judgmental and self-righteous hindering us from "bearing one another's burdens." To truly practice "ANOTHERINGS" we must pray to see each other through the eyes of God and His "AMAZING GRACE"! I still have a long way to go, so pray with me and for me as I pray with and for you, to God's glory and our good. This blog has been written against the background of dealing with up close and personal family tragedies!

INTIMACY!

INTIMACY: Defined means UP CLOSE AND PERSONAL or COMMUNICATION FACE TO FACE.

The Scriptures declare,

"Cast all your CARE upon GOD; for HE cares for you."

Thus, one word that best summarizes the mechanics of INTIMACY and reveals the great hunger for its reality in the heart of mankind is the word CARE! Each of its letters presents the power and glory of this small word which is the heartbeat of our greatest desire and need. Whether in marriage, friendships, family, neighbors, kin, marketplace or in the understanding and relationship with GOD the root of INTIMACY is SELFLESS CARE!

C = *COMPASSION* is a love not attached to sexual energy but is in lock step with another for the good of ANOTHER. A kind of love that feels and experiences the spirit and thinking of another with no strings attached. It thus grows a long term personal bond with another.

A = *AVAILABILITY* is the actual adjustment of one's life to accommodate another in their joy and pain. Availability is not always easy or simple but demands a readjustment of an individual's priorities and personal needs as one reaches out to another. Therefore, it is a choice expressed because of the concern and compassion for another. Availability is on call 24/7 as it is manifest in the maintenance of INTIMACY expressed in the SELFLESS CARING for another, regardless of the inconvenience or difficulty.

R = *REALITY* comprises a relationship with God or another in real time. INTIMACY demands that each person maintain their individuality as they interact with God or another. Thus, as we interact with another we must keep our REALITIES separate. In human relationships we must protect and never compromise the integrity of each person's reality. There is a tendency for the needy person in a relationship to become codependent on the strength of another. The truth of the matter is we all in our relationships are from time to time the "needy one" becoming codependent. Codependency is a disease that only gets worse if it is not identified and dealt with. The realities of both people in a relationship must protect their own identity as they CARE for ONE ANOTHER. INTIMACY between people is maintained by each living inside their own REALITY, thus allowing each person to be who they are manifesting compassion and growth in their CARING FOR ONE ANOTHER over time.

E = *ENDURANCE* is an ultimate necessity of INTIMACY as it manifests itself in SELFLESS CARING. Time proves and tests the authenticity of INTIMACY as it ENDURES the highs and lows of life. One of the fruit of the Holy Spirit is long-suffering. The character of INTIMACY is best revealed in our lives by its power to suffer long with another as a giver not a taker. Thus, revealing how GOD endures or suffers long with us in our faith journey. Our greatest INTIMACY with GOD grows out of our hurt pain and brokenness as HE walks with us THRU IT ALL.

No matter how far we wander HE welcomes us home as HE did the prodigal son of Scripture. Our wanderings as believers take us away from fellowship with the FATHER, not our relationship. GOD holds HIS children close to HIS heart ever ready to restore fellowship's INTIMACY. Exampling to us how we as believers should suffer long with one another with SELFLESS CARE building true INTIMACY, casting all our CARES on JESUS THE AUTHOR AND FINISHER OF OUR FAITH BEARING ONE ANOTHER'S BURDENS AND FULFILLING THE LAW OF CHRIST. Such INTIMACY cannot be faked.

JESUS AIN'T FOR SALE!

I weary at all the unholy junk for sale! Pictures, statues, bookmarks, bumper stickers, lapel pins, novelties, odds and ends of every description. It's unending. Music, Bibles, and books for study can feed our GROWING IN GRACE, but also feeds our itch for religious God stuff. Consumerism has too often conquered our thinking in this culture. Jesus is not a religious icon or rock star, but Emmanuel, "GOD WITH US"! He died for us to live in us and work thru us "on the basis of faith." He is not a commodity to be bought or sold. The gift of His righteousness is a gift offered freely to all out of the abundance of His love and grace.

No gimmicks! We confuse the unbeliever when we attach Jesus and His name to buildings, real estate, group names and "selling pressure" to get people "saved"! People are not pawns. Thus, the Jesus of history and promise is lost in the wilderness of religious hype.

I repeat what many others have said time and again: THE HOLY SPIRIT ALONE CONVICTS MANKIND OF THEIR NEED FOR GOD AND THEIR BROKENNESS. GOD ALONE JUDGES THE HEARTS OF HUMANITY, NOT US! FINALLY, AS AN

AMBASSADOR FOR CHRIST IT IS OUR COMMISSION AS BELIEVERS TO ALLOW GOD TO LOVE THROUGH US THOSE THAT HE LOVES "PERIOD"!

Thus, over a lifetime in "GRACE and KNOWLEDGE" we learn the work of GOD is to believe JESUS who GOD sent and allow HIM to LOVE through us! This is contrary to human nature. It is Christ in us the HOPE of glory. AMAZING GRACE HOW SWEET THE SOUND THAT SAVED A WRETCH LIKE ME!

JESUS SOUND BYTES

In this day of soundbites and small and simple packaging we often over speak. The teachings of JESUS CHRIST are simple and basic,

"FOLLOW ME,"

and

"LOSE YOUR LIFE FOR MY SAKE AND FIND IT,"

are two such declarations.

They need no lectures to explain them, for they are what they are. There are three aspects of the realities of CHRIST that help me keep it simple

"JESUS WEPT" – Jesus was called to the tomb of Lazarus and the shortest verse in all the Bible is "JESUS WEPT." No greater revelation of the HUMANITY of Jesus our Lord than the fact that he wept at the tomb of Lazarus. I did not say "He Cried" but "He Wept," a cry from the very depths of the human burden which He understood was all mankind's.

He knew the inner burden of the sin curse of mankind concerning death and dying. He wept from the inner reality of HIS HUMANITY that REVEALED HIS DEITY, not temporary tears of grief, but He WEPT knowing all that was to be found in mankind's burden of sin and death. Truly a profound statement of HIS HUMANITY, revealing His knowledge of our real pain!

Remember John's statement,

> "BEHOLD THE LAMB OF GOD who takes away the sin of the world."

"IT IS FINISHED" – The work of CHRIST on the CROSS in our behalf brought the old economy of the law to a conclusion in fulfillment. The veil in the temple was rent from top to bottom and fell away so that we may now "come boldly to the throne of grace." We now stand before "Holy God" wrapped in the COMPLETED WORK OF CHRIST in payment for our sin "by HIS stripes we are healed, delivered, or saved," by the shedding of HIS BLOOD on the CROSS in our behalf.

Our relationship to GOD is based on "done" not do and don't do, which equal do-do, HIS PROVISION NOT OUR PERFORMANCE is the message. The good news is GOD'S work in our behalf. "IT IS FINISHED" and his righteousness is now a GIFT freely given to all who believe, thus receiving the "ABUNDANCE OF HIS GRACE." Truly on the CROSS a revelation of both THE HUMANITY AND THE DEITY OF JESUS CHRIST shines in a dark world.

"HE IS RISEN" – The full message of the Gospel is JESUS died, buried and rose from the dead, and if He was NOT RAISED we "have no hope and all is in vain." When speaking in a small village in India I declared, "HE IS RISEN from the dead, "GOOD NEWS." In their language I heard a response in unison from the crowd which I did not understand until my interpreter declared, they are shouting at you "GOOD NEWS."

The message of the cross finds it's finality in the RESURRECTION, a full revealing of HIS DEITY. HIS HUMANITY UNTARNISHED / HIS DEITY UNDIMINISHED! The KISS OF LIFE IS IN JESUS CHRIST ALONE and the proof is in the POWER OF THE GOSPEL, which brings LIFE AND LIFE ABUNDANTLY. No religion or philosophy could ever do this. May we all declare before our world, WE WOULD SEE JESUS!

NO GOODY GOODIES!

Charlotte Elliott, 1789-1871, wrote the following lines from the song "Just As I AM" which declares my feelings that night at 16 years old when I understood and trusted the message of God's grace, as a student at Hampden Dubose Academy in Florida.

> "Just as I am, though tossed about
> With many a conflict, many a doubt,
> Fightings and fears within, without,
> O Lamb of God, I come, I come."

Over the years I had rebelled against the term "good and bad Christian." I now understand that such a statement is not a Biblical concept and is a turn off to anyone who might consider the claims of Christ. The truth of Scripture is a matter of "weak and strong" which can be realized in a believer at any time. The very reality of Jesus Christ in our lives sets up a conflict between our old "carnal" nature and the "righteousness of God" which brings salvation and options of an eternal nature, declared as "the just shall live by faith." The natural man has no such struggle, "not understanding the things of God" nor its work in his or her life.

As a "church kid" I thought that I wanted to be a "good

Christian" so as to be truly religious and proper among the people who called the plays. It didn't take me long to realize that being good was not my thing. The Scripture I discovered declares that "none are good" and that our righteousness is as a "filthy rag." Thus, I learned to "act like a Christian" whatever was determined by the group I was with at the time. I really learned to be an actor and a poor one at that. After a serious confrontation with the Gospel for the first time at 16, I began to search the Scripture for myself, discovering I was never commanded to be good and not bad. Good was used for deeds and works toward others, not my own doing. Goodness is a fruit of the Spirit of God by which we as believers are empowered to do "good works"!

Eventually "Spiritual Maintenance" would come from a verse which commanded to "maintain good works for they are good and profitable for men"! No command to do them to gain the approval of God but to impact others. I discovered that there were no bad questions, but that I had been given bad answers from which Scripture began to set me free. I began to grasp the truth that believers deal with being weak because of our connection to our flesh, and strong as it relates to our relation to the Holy Spirit who lives within us. Thus, the hard reality was that our flesh is vulnerable and weak within our inner man but is enabled by the Holy Spirit to be strong. Thus, we are "born to war." Self-righteousness has no place in the life of the believer, but when we posture and create the appearance of piety and being a "goodie two-shoes or holy Joe" we fool ourselves and disconnect from hurting, unbelieving people.

Paul the apostle declared that when he was weak, he was strong. When we become all things to all men that we might win them, we must have bigger ears and a smaller mouth, humbly walking in big shoes. Our holiness is our "wholeness empowered by the "Holy Spirit" as "temples of the "Holy Spirit" who lives within us. God does not live in buildings made with hands, period. Jesus Christ, came into the world in a baby's skin, born of a virgin, died, buried and rose from the dead that we might have everlasting life and here and now "life abundantly."

Thus, the "gift of His righteousness" is a gift to all who will trust Him. It is freely given, and we receive His love and grace by faith alone. We therefore declare by faith that we are an imperfect, greatly loved, and forgiven child of God, sometimes weak and sometimes strong. Jesus said we should let our light shine before others that they can see our good works and glorify our Father in heaven.

GRACE DRIVEN LIFE!

G *GOSPEL* = The Death, Burial and Resurrection of Jesus in payment for our sin debt. Good News!

R *RIGHTEOUSNESS RECONCILIATION AND REDEMPTION* = Jesus became our sin for us and gave us the gift of His righteousness, Reconciling and Sealing us with the Holy Spirit until the day of Redemption, when we leave these bodies and transfer to the FATHER'S heaven.

A *ATONEMENT* = Jesus death on the Cross by the shedding of His blood, HE became the perfect substitute and sacrifice in full payment for our sin debt.

C *COMMUNION* = We come BOLDLY to the THRONE of GRACE in prayer and thanksgiving because of the Cross and the Resurrection.

E *ENDURANCE* = Jesus ENDURED His suffering empowering us that we may ENDURE all things. The acrostic that has been used often for defining grace is God's Righteousness At Christ's Expense. The law came by Moses, but grace and truth by Jesus the Christ.

AGAPE-LOVE IS ONE OF A KIND UNCONDITIONAL

LOVE. This GRACE-LOVE is not the norm for mankind who is given to vengeance, and a return of like behavior when wronged.

GRACE was not a word or reality created by men and their gods throughout the history of man. It is not a religious word but a word from the same intelligence that created gravity and the physics of the universe. This GRACE stands in judgment of the evil and criminality of mankind while at the same time loving mankind.

GRACE is not magic but an intelligent, unconditional, determined love and forgiveness ordained by an intelligence that is greater than its creation and the creature, capable of thought, design and giving life. Finally, GRACE is not a religion or philosophy but a power that can drive man to be greater than flesh and blood and empower those who receive it.

Thus, by HIS power we are salvaged by faith as this GRACE is manifest by agape-love, this one of a kind unconditional LOVE which is GOD revealed. Jesus declared "that God is a Spirit and those who worship Him worship Him in Spirit and in Truth."

Scriptures declare GOD IS LOVE.

"For GOD so LOVED the world, that he gave his only begotten ONE OF A KIND SON, (Jesus) that whosoever

believes on Him would not perish but, have eternal life."

"No man has seen GOD at any time; the only begotten Son, (JESUS) who is in the bosom of the Father, GOD has declared HIM."

THEREFORE, JESUS IS HUMANITY UNTARNISHED AND DEITY UNDIMINISHED. THUS, AS BELIEVERS WE ARE SALVAGED, DRIVEN AND SUSTAINED BY GOD'S LOVE REVEALED BY HIS AMAZING GRACE.

BROKEN WORLD! / BROKEN ME!

TO BE OR NOT TO BE: In our world of broken dreams and broken hearts we are commanded to "Bear one another's burdens and fulfill the law of Christ"! As believers in Jesus death, burial and resurrection we are commissioned to be SALT AND LIGHT, both quiet but powerful witnesses to God's grace. I cannot fix anybody but offer them the same grace that found me and gave me the "GIFT OF GOD'S RIGHTEOUSNESS" when I hurt so bad and was so confused.

We live in a world of darkness and deception and should pray daily that we can make a difference one person at a time as we manifest God's light and love to His glory and our good. We pray daily for wisdom and discernment in a broken and divided world that we cannot fix, that God will shine His light in and through us one day at a time to one person at a time thus making a difference in our personal world by being salt and light.

BE SALT IN A TASTELESS WORLD! LET YOUR LIFE BE A SALTY TREAT / MAKING OTHERS THIRST FOR THE WATER OF LIFE / JUST A FEW GRAINS OF SALTY GRACE WILL BRING FLAVOR TO YOUR CONVERSATIONS AND YOUR ACTIONS

/ REMEMBER, TOO MUCH SALT CHOKES; MEASURE THE SALT OF GRACE WITH LOVE AND COMPASSION / SO BE SALT! / BE LIGHT BY BEING REAL IN YOUR WALK WITH THE LORD! / BE SPIRITUAL IN NATURAL MATTERS AND NATURAL IN SPIRITUAL MATTERS / LIGHT IS QUIET / IT MANIFESTS ITSELF IN CARING ATTITUDES AND SIMPLE ACTS OF KINDNESS / OPENING DOORS FOR YOUR LIGHT TO SHINE / SO BE LIGHT!

Over the years of my life there is one word that has defined my life time after time. This word is BROKEN and as a child it often brought much grief to my life. My favorite toy was BROKEN because I tore it apart to fix it. My mother's favorite vase was BROKEN by my carelessness. My allowance spent, BROKE. As I got into my teens I BROKE my parent's hearts by misdeeds. Teenager's love BROKE up. Marriages BROKE apart. Delinquency and laws were BROKEN. Adult years bring BROKEN dreams, BROKEN health and BROKEN spirits into the human condition.

Thus, life reveals BROKENNESS at every level of the human experience. The word "lost" declares a BROKENNESS with eternal consequences. Therefore in finality, our BROKENNESS at every level of existence cries out for a remedy that restores, heals and fixes that which is BROKEN! Where do we go, who do we turn to?

We have so often failed ourselves and others also have failed to satisfy our burden and overwhelming need to be fixed, healed and delivered from the struggles and burdens of life.

A BROKEN heart demands relief as it defines itself by anger, self-righteousness, selfishness and self-pity. God alone comes to us with His love, grace and forgiveness even to the death of His Son on the cross, BROKEN AND SPILLED OUT for all of mankind. JESUS CHRIST DIED, WAS BURIED AND ROSE FROM THE DEAD TO GIVE US THE GIFT OF HIS RIGHTEOUSNESS.

We as believers can now declare, ONCE I WAS BROKEN AND UNDONE BUT NOW I SEE THE HEALING LIGHT OF GOD'S GRACE, I ONCE WAS LOST AND BROKEN BUT NOW I AM FOUND AND BEING ETERNALLY REPAIRED.

CALLED OUT ONES!

The CHURCH is an ekklesia, an assembly of God's people, called out from the world, never means a building. The English "church" derives for the Middle English "chirche" which is from the German "kirche," which is from the Greek "kuriakon," which sometimes means building, where early ecclesia worshipped, and came from "kurios," Lord or master," which in turn, came from "kuros" meaning "authority, supreme power." WILLIAM BARLOW

Out of this same mind set came the laity/clergy error that has forever infected the CHURCH. Peter set matters straight in the early church with the wonderful revelation of the "PRIESTHOOD OF THE BELIEVER," that is all believers are equal to each other, and given gifts of the Spirit by which the "EKKLESIA" (the called-out ones) are strengthened and grow in grace.

> "...CHRIST LOVED THE CHURCH (EKKLESIA – CALLED OUT ONES) AND GAVE HIMSELF UP FOR HER..."

> "...UPON THIS ROCK (KIND OF FAITH PETER REVEALED) I WILL BUILD MY CHURCH (EKKLESIA – CALLED OUT ONES)..."

> "FOR BY ONE SPIRIT (THE HOLY SPIRIT) WE WERE

BAPTIZED INTO ONE BODY (THE CHURCH) ...WE WERE ALL MADE (ALL BELIEVERS) TO DRINK OF ONE SPIRIT (THE HOLY SPIRIT)."

"I PRAY THAT THE EYES OF YOUR HEART MAY BE ENLIGHTENED, SO THAT YOU WILL KNOW WHAT IS THE HOPE OF HIS CALLING. WHAT ARE THE RICHES OF THE GLORY OF HIS INHERITANCE IN THE SAINTS, AND WHAT IS THE SURPASSING GREATNESS OF HIS POWER TOWARD US WHO BELIEVE, THERE ARE IN ACCORDANCE WITH THE WORKING OF THE STRENGTH OF HIS MIGHT WHICH GOD BROUGHT ABOUT IN CHRIST, WHEN HE RAISED HIM FROM THE DEAD AND SEATED HIM AT HIS RIGHT HAND IN HEAVENLY PLACES, FAR ABOVE ALL RULE AND AUTHORITY AND POWER AND DOMINION, AND EVERY NAME THAT IS NAMED, NOT ONLY IN THIS AGE (JEWISH AGE) BUT ALSO IN THE ONE TO COME. AND HE SHALL PUT ALL THINGS IN SUBJECTION UNDER HIS FEET AND GAVE HIM AS HEAD OVER ALL THINGS TO THE CHURCH, WHICH IS HIS BODY, THE FULLNESS OF HIM WHO FILLS ALL IN ALL."

"...WE, WHO ARE MANY, ARE ONE BODY IN CHRIST, AND INDIVIDUALLY MEMBERS ONE OF ANOTHER."

"LOVE ONE ANOTHER, EVEN AS I HAVE LOVED YOU, THAT YOU ALSO LOVE ONE ANOTHER. BY THIS ALL MEN WILL KNOW THAT YOU ARE MY DISCIPLES, IF YOU HAVE LOVE ONE FOR ANOTHER."

CHURCH IS NOT SOMEWHERE WE GO, BUT RATHER WHO WE ARE AND WHAT WE DO OUT OF THE OVERFLOW OF OUR DAILY WALK. I GREW UP GOING TO CHURCH MEETINGS EVERY TIME THE DOORS WERE OPENED. I WAS MARRIED TO THE PROGRAMS AND THE PROCESS, WHILE ALL THE TIME MEASURING MY SPIRITUALITY BY MY INVOLVEMENT IN THEM, RATHER THAN GOD'S GRACE.

TODAY THERE ARE HUNDREDS OF GROUPS UNDER DIFFERENT NAMES CLAIMING TO BE THE ONLY ONE WITH THE TRUTH. MANY SPLIT OFF OF OTHER SPLITS BECAUSE OF METHODS, PERSONALITIES AND DIFFERING SHADES OF DOCTRINE. MANY TRAVEL UNDER THE SAME NAME WITH AN ADDED WORD TO DECLARE THEIR POINT OF DIFFERENCE. MANY SPEAK OF THEIR CHURCH, THEIR PASTOR AND THEIR PROGRAMS AS IF THEY POSSESSED THE ONLY WAY.

IN A CITY THE SIZE OF OURS, EVERY SHOPPING CENTER AND EVERY PART OF TOWN HAS MANY BUILDINGS AND PROPERTIES LABELED CHURCH. AS THE WORLD LOOKS ON, NO DOUBT MANY WOULD ASK WHERE IS THE REAL CHURCH? WHO IS RIGHT?

THE SCRIPTURE CLEARLY DECLARES THAT,

"THE GOD WHO MADE THE WORLD AND ALL

THINGS IN IT, SINCE HE IS LORD OF HEAVEN AND EARTH, DOES NOT DWELL IN TEMPLES MADE WITH HANDS."

AGAIN,

"THE MOST HIGH DOES NOT DWELL IN HOUSES (BUILDINGS) MADE BY HUMAN HANDS."

(ACTS 7:48)

FINALLY, THE TRUE HOUSE OF GOD OR TEMPLE OF GOD IS CLEARLY REVEALED,

"...DO YOU NOT KNOW THAT YOUR BODY IS A TEMPLE (GOD'S HOUSE) OF THE HOLY SPIRIT WHO IS IN YOU, WHOM YOU HAVE FROM GOD, AND THAT YOU ARE NOT YOUR OWN"?

"No man builds the CHURCH but CHRIST alone. Whoever is minded to build the CHURCH is surely on the way to destroying it; for he will build a temple to idols without wishing or knowing it. We must confess, HE builds; we must PROCLAIM HE builds; we must pray to HIM, that he may build. We do not know HIS plan. We cannot see whether HE is building or pulling down.

It may be that the times which by human standards are times of collapse are for HIM the greatest times of construction...it is a great comfort which CHRIST gives to HIS CHURCH; you confess, preach, bear witness to me; and I alone will build where it pleases me. Do not meddle in what is my province. Do what is given to you to do; do it well and you have done enough. But do it well.

Pay no heed to views, don't ask for judgments, don't always be calculating what will happen, don't be always on the lookout for another refuge! CHURCH STAY CHURCH; but CHURCH, confess, confess, confess! CHRIST alone is your LORD; from HIS grace alone, can you live. PROCLAIM CHRIST LIVES!"

Dietrich Bonhoeffer

God said,

"The light shining out of the darkness, has put in our hearts the light of the knowledge of the glory of God in the face of Jesus Christ,"

Scripture declares,

"Now those in Berea were more noble minded than those in Thessalonica, in that they received the Word with all readiness of the mind, examining the Scriptures daily, whether it was true. Bearing one another's burdens, and thus fulfilling the law of Christ."

EQUAL BUT DIFFERENT

Each believer in Jesus Christ is on a personal journey with each of us at a different place, with different issues, yet with similar struggles. No agreement necessary! The fight over agreement often leads to a keep face, an ego war! Argument and debate is not involved, but searching the scriptures to seek understanding, thus giving the Holy Spirit an opportunity to do His work in us in God's time without brain washing each other with a "cookie cutter" mentality. Who we believe is the issue more than what we believe.

As the WHO is established as our final authority, then what we believe grows out of that AUTHORITY. Humility is the mark of a maturing believer. True intimacy develops in a one on one, in your face relationship with ANOTHER.

Time together is absolutely essential. Find time, make time and take time to share hearts, mind and soul without fear of disclosure or intimidation.

Jesus declared,

> "Where two or three are gathered together in my name, there am I in the midst of them."

The believer's spiritual growth as the growth and development of a child demands intimacy, the very heart of nurturing. This is true of me having grown up all of my life as an insider of the "RELIGIOUS" if not always the people of God at least a "fan club."

As I look back over the years it appears far too much time was spent on buildings, monies and numbers. Every searching believer must have and crave at some point intimacy and nurture and an opportunity to ask questions and question answers.

We have often just taken for granted that it is the normal to just buy into a routine that offers very little space for "searching out the scriptures to see if they are so" in an environment of love without "dogma and judgment."

It is the Holy Spirit alone who came to "convict the world of sin, righteousness and judgment" and none of that has our signature on it. Thus, as we grow in grace and knowledge, with great humility the manifestation of God's grace manifests a "bearing one another's burden and fulfilling the law of Christ."

Every believer is equal to the other and we have different gifts to manifest in the body of Christ. We have created too often a caste system with "preachers on top" along with different religious orders next down the chain to just the regular "pew Christian." This is nonsense, we all are equal but with different gifts but the same relation to God as His children. God has no pets!

Each of us has the challenge and authority as called

of God, imperfect, sinful, undeserving, but redeemed, forgiven and greatly blessed children of God. The Scriptures are for each of us equally and the Holy Spirit alone our teacher. Thus, as we seek intimacy with others who are real and honest, sharing our hunger, we are nurtured and growing. Talking heads and faceless crowds will never produce intimacy.

"NO ONE CARES WHAT WE KNOW UNLESS THEY KNOW THAT WE CARE!" GROWING IN GRACE COMES AS WE DANCE CLOSE TO GOD AND HIS WORD SHARING HIS LOVE AND GRACE.

NATURAL LIFE!

In the world where I grew up, "DOING WHAT COMES NATURALLY" was our senseless answer to our odd behavior. My spiritual depth was "go to church deep" and I knew very little of grace and "being the church." Having fun was my game except for the occasional "conscience attack" and a walk down the church aisle for prayer. I had learned a ton of Scripture "by heart" but no mind or feet connected.

When my parents tired of my "doing what came natural" they pulled the rug out from under me and sent me to Hampden Dubose Academy, a private "Christian" boarding school in central Florida. There the Lord through faithful, imperfect people, both teachers and students, addressed my life.

Jesus Christ became a reality for the first time bringing not only a heartbeat but a hungry mind to know and be known by God's grace. No perfection ever came with my new life in Christ, which my religious past imagined but never realized. I had found God's grace, peace and joy. Just doing what came naturally was no longer acceptable and for the first time my sinful, rebellious heart received God's righteousness as a gift and rested in Him instead of in my silly, futile, infantile, self-righteousness, based on do and don't do.

> "The NATURAL MAN/WOMAN without the Spirit of God does not accept the things that come from the Spirit of God, for they are foolishness to him /her and they cannot understand them."

Scripture declares that

> "The HEART of man/woman is deceitful above all else, desperately wicked, and beyond cure, who can understand it"?

Natural men and women are given to living life out of bounds and missing the mark of God's purpose. Thus, at the age of 16 the Lord found me, and my life began a faith walk that forever changed my core. I had many questions and had been given many bad answers. I had a big problem with those who constantly railed against the natural man and his domain as if it could change mankind's heart. I realized that no matter how much one railed against the natural man's behavior it could not turn man/woman's heart to God.

Real repentance (a change of mind) comes only from the Holy Spirit who convicts of sin, righteousness and judgment. Salvation is from the Lord not man.

Scripture declares, that no man seeks God and that none are good, not even one. It is normal behavior for the natural man/woman to live loose and self-centered lives whose only authority is themselves. There are exceptions where the natural man/woman has good values without reference to God.

The structured, ordered life produces some wonderful successful people and even moral people, without the hope and peace generated by God's love and grace. Also, those who make their own way no matter how successful, fall into the trap of denying the possibility of knowing God, leading to a religion of self-sufficiency and arrogance.

Many natural people who have no concern for Scripture and the inner hunger for God, are drawn to religion, a false substitute. Religion puts emphasis on human PERFORMANCE while God's grace is about His PROVISION and His POWER. Salvation and faith in God is not ours to give.

AS WE MANIFEST OUR RELATIONSHIP TO GOD IN A TROUBLED WORLD WE MUST LEARN TO BE NATURAL IN SPIRITUAL MATTERS AND SPIRITUAL IN NATURAL MATTERS WITH LOVE AND GRACE!

COMMONALITY

Life is a JOURNEY, unpredictable as the wind, often filled with mystery and adventure, comedy and tragedy. It is never boring unless we bog down in the process and lose our way.

The word LOST defines man, without a purpose, direction, nor a compass to guide him/her. When one trusts in Jesus Christ on the basis of faith by grace's empowerment, he/she discovers a whole new world that God ordains.

Each individual believer is special, the product of many influences that compose our life. There are five major concerns that form our individuality and thus a JOURNAL OF OUR COMMONALITY!

CHEMISTRY – The genetic formula that formed us is composed of many factors, some known and some unknown. Our personal DNA is comprised of our ancestry that carries certain genes forward, often skipping generations and manifesting certain abilities that were not seen in later generations of a family. Our mother and father bring their own particular and peculiar genes that compose a whole new person, with potentials, strengths and weaknesses.

CONDITIONING – The second major factor that

contributes to our JOURNEY and forms our early thinking about LIFE is conditioning. During our first years we adapt so many ways of thinking about life, our sexuality, spirituality, life style, boundaries and how we understand right and wrong. The die is cast early and only God can alter the course once it is set, though instructions and discipline can produce changes. Behavior and patterns of thought fill the once blank tape of our life.

CULTURE – It doesn't take a psychiatrist to see how we all have been greatly influenced by our culture. In my travels I have seen time and again that each culture displays itself through its children. Certain patterns are repeated and manifest generation after generation, setting up traditions and forms of morality or immorality peculiar to the values of the day. Culture norms are very fluid and given to change depending on the influences of the time. I am reminded daily that this culture today is not the culture I grew up with.

CIRCUMSTANCES – As we move from childhood into adolescence and adulthood we deal with the reality of personal pain and emotional hurt, handling life's circumstances by falling back on the process lived out by our family and peers. It is a blessing to have a personal relationship with God and a "faith force" so as to view life through His plan and purpose for our lives and move beyond our initial conditioning and the surrounding culture so as to cope with life's ups and downs. Every person has their share of the good, the bad and the ugly, but it is how we deal with life's issues that make the difference.

CHOICES – The bottom line in the chain of influences on our lives is our personal choices. No doubt other influences carry weight, but the final matter is our choices. Our spirituality is a work of God's love and grace, a gift of His righteousness.

Our reception of this great miracle of love and grace is a choice. Life isn't a spectator sport but a continual, day by day interaction with light and darkness, righteousness and evil, and if we choose, God working in and through us to His glory and our good.

FOR SOME REASON WE ARE DIGITAL FRIENDS ON FACEBOOK, HAVING CROSSED PATHS IN OUR JOURNEY. MANY OF US HAVE NEVER MET FACE TO FACE AND OTHERS HAVE KNOWN ONE ANOTHER FOR YEARS, YET WE SHARE MANY OF THE SAME LIFE EXPERIENCES. WE FIND STRENGTH IN OUR MUTUAL STRUGGLES AND GROWTH BY TRUSTING GOD'S DIVINE

PROVIDENCE IN OUR LIVES. I LOVE YOU AND AM GLAD YOU ARE THERE.

SPIRITUAL FOOD!

FEEDING OUR NEW LIFE IN CHRIST IS OUR GREATEST CHALLENGE. Many of us were introduced somewhere in our faith journey with the idea that we should fight against our old nasty selfish nature, in order to grow in grace. This religious idea is not the teaching of Scripture but a concoction of those who think that sinful behavior and thinking can be overcome by fighting our selfish old nature and its desires! This is fruitless, leading us to a life of constant failure and little or no spiritual growth. Often lecturing or preaching has majored on the theme of fighting our old nature.

True victory over a lifetime is not the result of a single re-dedication, but a daily walk, one step at a time, by faith, feeding the new nature on God's love, grace and truth from the Scriptures empowered by the Holy Spirit.

The Scripture does not refer to believers as good or bad, but rather weak or strong! In any given time frame, we can find ourselves both weak and strong. Victory is found in our lives one minute at a time as we walk by faith, not by feelings, which come and go and are often driven by our hormones! Humbly, one moment at a time, we learn to seek God's presence and power in our walk, feeding ourselves on God's promises and provisions.

The life of faith is not built on our PERFORMANCE but GOD'S PROVISION. A daily quiet time, a moment of thanksgiving and prayer and readings from Scripture feeds our spiritual inner man. Do this instead of fighting our old selfish nature in a human, fleshly manner assuring us of failure.

Over a lifetime we daily face our "inability," discovering time and again that FEEDING THE NEW NATURE is indeed the way to moment by moment victory. It should never be a constant beating up the flesh, fighting our urges and failing, guilt-ridden and shamed by our inability and repeat offenses.

Thus, daily feeding our new "in Christ" relationship, confessing our sins and declaring thanks to God, who gives us the victory through our Lord Jesus Christ. WE WORK IN THE DARK AND WALK IN THE LIGHT!

FOCUS!

In the process of my daily FAITH WALK one word I pray for is FOCUS. This small word calls me back to center and prioritizes my life in a world of distractions. Scripture declares that a double minded man is unstable in all his ways. Multitasking is greatly prized in our technical world.

In our walk with the Lord,

> *"seeking first the kingdom of God and His righteousness,"*

is a command by JESUS the CHRIST to ALL believers.

We are an overly distracted and entertained people with many goodies to pull our minds and hearts away daily from what is most important. Therefore, I defined the powerful word FOCUS by spelling it out as follows:

F *FAITH* CONNECTS US WITH GOD'S GRACE. Both GRACE AND FAITH are gifts given by measure to each ONE who BELIEVES GOD'S WORD. The Scriptures by the power of the HOLY SPIRIT impregnates our minds and hearts empowering us to receive GOD'S love and grace and the gift of HIS RIGHTEOUSNESS thus CONNECTING us to the power of ETERNAL LIFE AND A FOCUS ON

ETERNAL VALUES.

O *OBEDIENCE* is responding to the truth of Scriptures by allowing the HOLY SPIRIT to guide us in our daily walk as we grow in grace and knowledge over a lifetime. This is a matter of CHOICE constantly confronting our old rebellious nature. Our daily interactions with SCRIPTURES encourage us as we CONFRONT daily CHOICES whether to OBEY or dance with broken feet. OBEDIENCE STRENGTHENS OUR FOCUS, thus our faithfulness. Failure to FOCUS does not take away our relationship with the FATHER but affects our FELLOWSHIP and renders us less effective in our WALK.

C *COMPASSION* is love that feels and reaches out to the needs of others, defined as CARE. The Holy Spirit is the power of God's LOVE indwelling us by faith, empowering us to BEAR ONE ANOTHERS BURDENS, FULFILLING THE LAW OF CHRIST. This is the precious FRUIT OF CONSISTENT FOCUS.

U *UNITY* in our FAITH WALK comes as truth and time works in our lives throughout our JOURNEY OF FAITH. Not only in our relationships with one another, but it CONFIRMS the UNITY of understanding within our inner man. FAITH truth moves from HEAD (knowledge), to HEART (understanding) and finally to our WALK (shoe leather). OUR WALK IS THE SALT AND LIGHT JESUS SAID WE WERE TO BE. This will be the source of our warfare over a lifetime as GOD'S TRUTH confronts our old rebellious, selfish nature. SCRIPTURE AND THE HOLY SPIRIT will daily address our inconsistencies and CONFIRM our FOCUSED WALK.

S *SCRIPTURE* is GOD'S CLEANING AGENT and the bottom line of a focused life. SCRIPTURE declares "the Lord is my strength" and as our strength we can proclaim, "God is our refuge and STRENGTH, a very present HELP in trouble." It is the Scriptures that give us VICTORIES and CLEAN our lives of the CORRUPTIONS of our minds and hearts, as we FOCUS DAILY on the CROSS, the BURIAL and the RESURRECTION of JESUS the CHRIST and HIS PROMISES AND PROVISIONS ON OUR BEHALF.

In this broken, hurting world filled with anger, violence, apathy and religious nonsense we as BELIEVERS must FOCUS AND REFOCUS moment by moment as we deal daily with life's many distractions and deceptions.

MY DAILY PRAYER AFTER GIVING THANKS FOR GOD'S LOVE AND GRACE IS "LORD PROTECT ME

FROM MYSELF AND KEEP ME FOCUSED ON YOUR PROMISES AND PROVISIONS SO THAT I WILL MAKE A DIFFERENCE IN MY WORLD AND INDIVIDUAL LIVES TO YOUR GLORY AND MY GOOD."

SCRIPTURE SEARCH!

"NOW THESE IN BEREA WERE MORE NOBLE THAN THOSE IN THESSALONICA, IN THAT THEY RECEIVED THE WORD WITH ALL READINESS OF THE MIND, EXAMINING THE SCRIPTURES DAILY, WHETHER THESE THINGS WERE SO."

"Bear one another's burdens, and so fulfill the law of Christ."

SPIRITUAL INTIMACY RULES.

Each believer in Jesus Christ is on a personal journey with each person at a different place, with different issues, yet with like struggles. No agreement necessary! The fight over agreement often leads to a keep face, ego war! Argument and debate is not involved but searching the Scriptures to see if they are so, giving the Holy Spirit an opportunity to do His work in God's time without brain washing each other with a "cookie cutter" mentality.

Who we believe is the issue more than what we believe. As the Who is established as the final authority then what we believe grows out of that authority.

Humility is the mark of a maturing believer. True intimacy develops in a one on one in your face relationship allowing each to face the other. Time together is absolutely essential. Find time, make time and take time to share your heart, mind and soul without fear of disclosure or intimidation.

JESUS said

> *"Where two or three are gathered together in my name there am I in the midst of them."*

The believer's spiritual growth, as the growth and development of a child demands intimacy, the very heart of nurturing.

As I look back over the years it appears far too much time has been spent on real estate, and buildings. Each believer must have intimacy and nurture, an opportunity to ask questions and question answers.

Somehow we have often just taken for granted that it is the normal to just buy into a routine that offers very little space for "searching out the Scriptures to see if they are so" in an environment of love without dogma and judgment.

It is the Holy Spirit alone who came to "convict the world of sin, righteousness and judgment" and none of that has our signature on it. Then we believers should grow in grace and knowledge, with great humility allowing the manifestation of God's grace by "bearing one another's burden and fulfilling the law of Christ."

Every believer is equal to the other and we each have different gifts to manifest in the body of Christ. We have created too often a caste system with "preachers on top" along with different religious orders on down the chain ending with just the regular "pew Christian." This is pure nonsense; we all are equal with different gifts but the same relation to God as His children, and God Has No Pets!

Each of us has the same challenge and authority as called of God, imperfect, sinful, undeserving, but redeemed, forgiven and greatly blessed children of God. The Scriptures are for each of us equally and they Holy alone our teacher. Thus we must seek our intimacy with others who will abide by the need in each to be real and honest, sharing our hunger.

Talking heads and faceless crowds will never produce intimacy. Sitting in pews back to back will never do more than allow us to be distracted by hair styles, clothes, ears, head shapes, and bodies of all sizes and shapes.

Lectures and sermons can indeed evangelize with a clear message but growth and nurture demands "face to face" time. Seek out one, two or a dozen to gather with you on a regular basis just to listen to each other and seek answers from God's Word without pressure in an environment of love, patience, care and a hungry heart.

When I was teaching college kids I always at the first session wrote on the board, "NO ONE CARES WHAT YOU KNOW UNLESS THEY KNOW THAT YOU CARE!" We who taught pastors and people in India learned that this need for intimacy and closeness is universal and essential too!

DANCE CLOSE TO GOD AND ONE ANOTHER DAILY AS YOU GROW IN GRACE. Your many responses to the blogs encourage me to keep on growing and sharing, in a real sense you nurture me.

Scripture declares,

> *"As for you, the Spirit which he gave you is still in you and you have no need of any teacher; but as his Spirit gives you teaching about all things true and not false, keep your hearts in him through the teaching which He has given you."*

THE HOLY SPIRIT IS OUR PRIMARY TEACHER WHEREAS WE BELIEVERS ARE GIFTED TO BRING FORWARD SCRIPTURE TO ONE ANOTHER SO THAT THE HOLY SPIRIT CAN AND WILL DO HIS PERFECT WORK IN US IN GOD'S TIME. CHOOSE

TO SEARCH AND GROW!

TEAM JESUS!

Competition is not in itself evil, but can do great harm and become an idol. In the arena of sports it is a driving force. For those of us who view it as fans it becomes a great source of entertainment and community. The down side is it can become a religion and create fanaticism and anger.

On ministry beach trips over the years we divided into teams for duties, skits and sports creating competition and fun with the objective of winning approval or prizes. The dark side of "TEAM SPIRIT" and competition when applied to our spiritual inner man is divisive and defeating. Scripture declares that as believers we should not compare ourselves with others thus being without understanding.

The tragedy of the "ONLY WE GOT IT RIGHT TEAM" is the hundreds of divisions, denominations and TEAM SPIRIT. We are to look to JESUS alone as the author and finisher of our faith and the only mediator between God and mankind as commanded by Scripture. Thus in our faith journey we are in competition with no one else.

THE JESUS OF SCRIPTURE AND HISTORY HAS BEEN DIVIDED INTO BITS & PIECES! Mankind is still dividing JESUS AND HIS PROPERTY at the foot of the cross as the day HE died. The ground at the foot of the cross is level. God has no pets; the lost the lonely and least finds rest in JESUS on the basis of faith only.

My sin and your sin meet GOD'S righteousness at the cross where we surrender our sinfulness and brokenness to the gift of HIS righteousness. Amazing GRACE is offered to all who will receive it FREELY GIVEN. No other team name or personality matters; JUST GIVE ME JESUS. He alone is the way, the truth and the life. He found me hiding, naked and afraid just as our original parents in Eden's garden, in rebellion and disobedience.

WE ALL HAVE SINNED, HE SEEKS US AND FINDS US AND GIVES US HIS LOVE AND FORGIVENESS. THUS I CAN DECLARE THAT I AM NOW AN IMPERFECT BROKEN VESSEL, A LOVED AND FORGIVEN CHILD OF GOD. A MEMBER OF "TEAM JESUS" ONLY! UNDESERVED AND UNMERITED, SIGNED ON BY JESUS, A COVENANT OF BLOOD SIGNED AND SEALED ON THE "OLD RUGGED CROSS" AND "HE IS RISEN." There is "NO COMPETITION" EVER!

THOUGHTS ARE THINGS!

Years ago someone said to me "THOUGHTS ARE THINGS"! Over the years I have pondered that thought and realized that thinking is apparently hard work and processing thought is a worthy daily activity. Perhaps in the realm of thinking we abort daily many great ideas that started as a thought, while some thoughts need to be aborted immediately. The ultimate test of thought is whether it puts shoes on or not.

The Scripture declares,

"As a man thinks within himself so is he"!

A thought can become an action, then a habit, even a character, and finally destiny. The old guys used to say when one appeared to be in deep thought or daydreaming, "A penny for your thoughts," calling us to give an answer to what we were thinking.

Paul the apostle talked about "taking every thought captive to the obedience of Christ"! Here again the greatest battle within ourselves is in our thought life and it is the most private and personal of all matters.

Perhaps our thoughts are nobody's business, but once they put shoes on and begin to walk, they sooner or later are seen by all. It appears that all great accomplishments started with a thought, perhaps all great evil begins with a small seed in one's thoughts.

Daily in my personal struggle within my mind I have encountered the good, the bad and the ugly of life. A virtual battlefield which demands in the language of today one of the following, "file, delete, print"! Once printed so to speak it is then public domain and certain actions are forthcoming.

The very copy of words on Facebook reflects where our mind is and our thoughts. Once they are printed on paper or the electronic tablet they are forever a witness to our thinking and perhaps our doings. In one sense when we become a part of social media we address our world in one way or another with words and thoughts that can never be called back. They are history and we must always live with it.

Before God we daily walk with all that we think and are laid out before Him so that I must to myself be true and to Him forever accountable! Words are like feathers blown in the wind, they can never be called back.

Truly our "thoughts are things." I share the newsletter and blogs to reveal not only to others but to myself those things which are at the core of my being. This is a real form of self-discovery and spiritual inventory of my own life. I pray that all of us will daily re-examine our lives and it all starts with our "THOUGHTS"! There is no greater intimacy than to share our thoughts with one another! Thanks for being in my life and sharing your thoughts!

VICTIM OR VICTOR

It is a truth that in our journey we struggle with the old sin nature which appears to dominate the believer, controlled for the most part by our old nature. Though the experience of our sin nature is common to all of us, it is not the life of faith desired by God for His children. I call it the victim cycle where we fall prey again and again to our old patterns and habits.

We should have from the first day of our new life in Christ been given insight to the war between the old and new nature in us. We would have been prepared as a new creature in Christ to deal properly with the war between the flesh and Spirit so that we could contend with the victim cycle without giving up and living in guile, all the days of our lives. The truth is as we grow in grace, we daily confront both victim and victory of daily life.

Though this is a probability, the norm must never be the victim cycle thus allowing it to become our comfort zone. Choosing to press on to maturity through the daily practice of seeking "solid food which is for the mature whose senses are trained to discern good and evil through practice." Jesus is a truth always and forever in our adventure of faith, "Christ in YOU the hope of glory."

Christ alone is our VICTORY and as we mature in our walk we learn to walk by faith not by feelings and thus we become more consistent and stable, not trusting in our flesh at all. It is obvious that this war would not even exist if we had not come to the knowledge of Jesus Christ, which set up a defense against the old nature. The issue is not whether or not as a believer we have a constant conflict between our old and new natures, but whether or not we are properly to live in VICTORY and not ever the lifestyle of a VICTIM as a child of God.

The life of Faith is based upon the promises of God. The Scriptures are all about the nature and character of God, His promises and integrity. The words covenant and testament have to do with His promises with man and God's track record of fulfilling what He promised. We are simply asked to trust God's promises and be thankful. My daily prayer consists of thanksgiving for God's faithfulness and help for those people and matters I pray for myself, daily that God will protect me from myself and others from me as well.

The next major understanding that we must grow into is that our relationship to God the Father is not established by our righteousness but His. Thus His Son, the Lord Jesus Christ is the source of our righteousness. "God put our sins on Jesus and gave us the righteousness of Christ as a free gift." Our performance is never the issue but rather God's.

Self-righteousness is absolutely of no avail and creates in us a religious, pious, arrogant spirit. The Scriptures declare that all our righteousness is as filthy rags and counts for nothing. The Holy Spirit works in us over a lifetime to empower us to live a life of faith which is impossible for the natural man.

We persevere because He preserves us, that is He keeps us patiently, even in our moments of carnality and war with our old nature, ever drawing us back, and teaching us through His Word and our life experiences, to REBOUND to His glory. He brings judgment on our sins by allowing us to experience the emptiness of our sins and returning to renewed fellowship. It is out of the abundance of His love and grace revealed in the person of Jesus Christ that gives us the victory and continually reminds us that He is able when we are not. We must always walk by faith, not feelings and trust His provision.

Charles H. Spurgeon, a pastor in England in the 1800 and 1900s revealed a letter in one of his many books from his nephew, about how he struggled in his walk with the Lord and how he prevailed:

My Dear Uncle,

I groan daily under a body of sin and corruption. Oh, for the time when I shall drop this flesh and be free from sin! I become more and more convinced that to attempt to be saved by a mixed covenant of works and faith is in the words of Berridge, "to yoke a snail with an elephant."

I desire to press forward for direction to my Master in all things; but as to trusting to my own obedience or righteousness, I should be worse than a fool and ten times worse than a madman. Poor dependent creatures!

Prayer had need be our constant employment; the foot of the throne our continual dwelling-place; for the Rock of Ages is our only safe Hiding-place. I rejoice in an assured knowledge by faith of my interest in Christ, and of certainty of my eternal salvation. Yet what strivings, what conflicts, what dangers and what enemies stand in my way!

The foes in my heart are so strong, that they would have killed me and sent me to hell long ere this, had the Lord left me; but blessed be His name! On my bended knees I have often to cry for succor and bless His name! I rejoice that the promises left on record are meant for me as well as for every saint of His, and such I desire to grasp them.

I glory in the distinguishing grace of God, and will not by the grace of God, step one inch from my principles, or think of adhering to the present fashionable sort of religion. But when I serve God, I find my old deceitful heart, full of the very essence of my old nature, rising up into my mouth, polluting all I say and do.

May we be enabled to trust the Lord, for He will help us; we must conquer; we cannot be lost, Lost! Impossible! For who is able to snatch us Out of the Father's hand?

May the Lord bless you exceedingly.

Your affectionate Nephew

WHAT GOD LOOKS LIKE!

We live in a broken world and agreement is not required. My blogs are a part of my continued search and struggle with the nature and character of God in a world of religious smoke and mirrors, and dog and pony shows. This is a heavy blog dealing with my own attempt to address myself and my culture with biblical authority desiring that we all open our minds to critical thinking as the Bereans of old "searching the Scriptures to see whether they are so."

Thus I return again and again to certain themes that daily challenge my world, where cheap ritualized religion has often replaced the miracle and power of "Amazing Grace."

The Scriptures declare,

> *"Oh the depth of the riches both of the wisdom and knowledge of God! For who has known the mind of the Lord, or who became his counselor? Or who has first given to Him that it might be paid back to Him again? For from Him and through Him and to Him are all things. To Him be glory forever."*

Jesus declared,

> *"He who has seen me has seen the Father; how can you say, show us the Father"?*

GOD LOOKS LIKE HIS NAME!

"God highly exalted Him (JESUS), and bestowed on Him the name which is above every name, so at the name of Jesus every knee will bow, of those who are in heaven and on earth and under the earth, and that every tongue will confess that Jesus Christ is Lord, to the glory of God the Father."

SPELLING GOD'S NAME!

G *GRACE* – LORD JESUS CHRIST / G GOD'S SKIN! (once visible TRUTH IN SKIN / now invisible / active)

O *ORDER* – HOLY SPIRIT GOD'S VOICE! (invisible / inaudible / active)

D *DESIGNER* – FATHER /THE MIND OF GOD! (invisible / active)

What's in a name? Let all the earth praise Him for His name is forever; it is His glory. The chief end of man is to know God, enjoy Him and rejoice! DO NOT BUILD MEMORIALS TO OPINIONS; rather allow the Holy Spirit to teach you over a lifetime WHO HE IS, AS YOU WALK BY FAITH!

CURIOSITY!

CURIOSITY? It is a desire to know or experience something. Two kinds of CURIOSITY have connected in my life over the years. The HOLY and the HORRID have clearly defined the spiritual warfare of my walk with the Lord. CURIOSITY is the same "inner itch" to know or experience the Adam and Eve syndrome. That is the choice between what God said and what we choose that pleasures us, called disobedience. We can declare this curiosity as HORRID because of its effects on our "spiritual balance."

Choices have consequences as Adam demonstrated in his choice to disobey God by eating the forbidden fruit, his disobedience plunging the human race into rebellion and chaos. All of our horrid self-serving desires though pleasurable for the moment, lead to hurt and regret.

The old saying "curiosity killed the cat" could be restated, "curiosity disappoints!" It was King David of old who after his tragic choices to commit adultery and murder prayed,

"I have sinned against God and Him alone."

Our horrid choices to pursue our pleasure bring great pain even after forgiveness, still bearing horrid fruit!

The confessing of our sin does not remove its consequences, but allows us to "walk in the light by the Spirit" restoring our fellowships.

The other side of CURIOSITY is the desire for the HOLY, which is a desire to know and experience the grace and righteousness of God. The Scripture introduces us to a little curious man named Zacchaeus who climbed up in a tree to see Jesus.

Once we are drawn to God's love and grace experiencing His salvation, our CURIOSITY about the wonder and power of the life of faith begins to grow. HOLY means separated unto God for His glory alone. Thus, a HOLY CURIOSITY empowered by the Holy Spirit draws us to JESUS CHRIST, the author and finisher of our faith, with a desire to grow in GRACE!

Therefore, CURIOSITY is both a positive and negative force in our lives and I have experienced both. Imagination in the human experience is also a positive and a negative essential to intellectual growth. It also can be used as a fantasy enhancer and attaching itself to our sexuality can initiate and feed temptation. Added to CURIOSITY it can make for harmful illusions and struggles.

We live in an age of "unbridled behavior" appealing to the "lust of the flesh"; fantasy which stimulates our

CURIOSITY. Often this effects how men and women see each other and skewing our sexuality. The porno and sex trade feed on human CURIOSITY and as believers we must constantly brush the teeth of our mind allowing the Holy Spirit the control of and renewing of our minds moment by moment.

The mind of Christ, His death, burial and resurrection demands constant awareness in our walk. A friend of mine when invited to look at lust material always said, "I can't, I am too weak to look"!

Thoughts are things and the father of acts and acts are the father of habits and habits are the father of a destiny.

IN FINALITY, OUR CURIOSITY CAN BE A HORRID MASTER OR A HOLY SERVANT, WE LIVE IN THE FLESH AND WAR IN THE SPIRIT. THE BELIEVER'S MIND IS REAL AND THE SPIRIT AND THE WORD ARE OUR ONLY WEAPONS! BE WARNED, BE ARMED! CHOICES!

WHISPERING HOPE!

"By the time we are grown, we have jobs and children; the noise of our lives has increased to such a level that we couldn't possible hear God because God rarely shouts - He whispers."

MIKE YACONELLI

Elijah in the Scripture had a confrontation with the prophets of Baal. Becoming very depressed he went into the desert to hide. God confronted him and Elijah pouted. God then sent Elijah to a mountain where He produced "a great and powerful wind which tore the mountains apart and shattered the rocks." God then sent an earthquake and a fire, and after the fire, "a still small voice," "a gentle whisper," "a sound of gentle blowing" or "a light murmuring sound." A missionary to Africa translated the passage, "a thin silence."

Much has been written about the "horse whisperer," a horse trainer who adopts a sympathetic view of the motives, needs, and desires of the horse based on natural horsemanship and equine psychology. The term as I understand it goes back to an Irish horseman who rehabilitated horses by standing face to face with a troubled horse, quietly speaking to the horse. Therefore the horse would be gentled by his techniques. Somehow it is the authority and the silent language between the whisperer and the animal that meets the need of the animal and remedies the problem.

As a kid I spent hours and years "doing church" and visiting many forms of "doing church." Religious forms and the lack of change in the lives of many including myself puzzled me. It often produced guilt about not doing enough, giving enough or being enough.

The message of "do and don't do" too often produced more guilt than grace. Process and ritual often seem more important than quietness and rest in the marvelous love and grace of our Heavenly Father, who provides all things for believers without reservation. Often "going to and doing church" became more about obligation, fighting sin and the old nature instead of feeding the new nature God's precious truths and BEING "the Church."

We were often told to "act like a Christian." Out of expectation and guilt we would do Oscar winning performances at "acting" instead of "growing in grace"! Scripture declares "be still and know that I am God."

The worship of God is a LIFESTYLE, not a momentary performance. Jesus reminded the woman at the well that some worship God here and others there, but "God is a Spirit and those who worship Him, worship Him in Spirit and Truth." Thus, true worship is a lifestyle of being who we are in Christ 24/7.

"Christ in you the hope of Glory" is the heart of worship and praise, at home, work and every aspect of the human experience. Worship is no longer a drama of promise, at a certain place and at a certain time, but a daily celebration. The Holy Spirit is indeed the quiet, "God Whisperer" addressing the INNER MAN. All believers are equal at the foot of the CROSS and at the EMPTY TOMB as we listen to our WHISPERING HOPE!

WORTH-SHIP

Worship is a lifestyle not an event! It is a matter of giving WORTH AND HONOR to an object or a subject on a continual basis. Jesus said WORSHIP of God is based on Spirit and Truth. Thus true worship is not about feelings or circumstances but a connection with GOD'S GRACE which endures life's highs and lows. It is the daily ups and downs that test our metal and tries our souls. Our ABIDING IN CHRIST is the source of our strength and our WORSHIP! Abiding IN CHRIST is the root of our Worship and we are the vine.

Our hormonal emotional self is common to the human condition. As believers in God's love and grace we live in bodies that are limited, fragile transporters of life in this dimension. Scriptures declare flesh and blood will not inherit the kingdom of God. Absent from the body present with the Lord. Our worship is not something worked up by "zealous cheerleaders" and a "spirited crowd," but a work of the Holy Spirit in life's daily grind.

Public worship is not to be discounted but can become an overpowering "crowd energized" experience that lacks the intimacy of private interactions with God and HIS WORD in "quietness and meditation" as He speaks and we listen.

"BE STILL AND KNOW THAT I AM GOD,"

declares Scripture.

Our greatest asset as believers is HUMILITY out of which true worship flows. Fleshly emotional stimulation is not the true source of worship but rather the HOLY SPIRIT, not a hyped-up self. All of us live daily between life's nitty-gritty, human negativity and counting blessings.

The ultimate manifestation of our WORSHIP is loving others and bearing their burden, not a personal emotional euphoria. This is also the greatest source of our joy. Not about the pulpit, the platform or public performance but the power and purpose of God and His provision daily in our walk. THUS WORSHIP IS A LIFESTYLE OF ANOTHERING TO GOD'S GLORY AND OUR GOOD, NOT A SELFIE EVENT!

CHOOSING LIFE

I've had choices
Since the day that I was born
There were voices
That told me right from wrong
If I had listened
No I wouldn't
Be here today
Living and dying
With the choices I made

I guess I'm payin'
For the things that I have done
If I could go back
Oh, Lord knows I'd run
But I'm still losin'
This game of life I play
Living and dying
With the choices I made

WRITTEN BY GEORGE JONES / COUNTRY MUSIC ARTIST WHO DIED A BELIEVER AND A CHANGED LIFE! (YOUTUBE GEORGE JONES "CHOICES")

God's likeness after which we were created gave us the capacity for CHOICES. His love for mankind desired for us to fulfill His purpose in creation. God's anger and wrath has always been revealed in His hatred of those things which corrupt and destroy MANKIND. He built into our world at creation all that we would need, to have a fulfilled life. We were never meant to be robots, but given the ability to CHOOSE, love or hate, good or evil. He gave His Spirit to empower us, and His Word to guide us for His Righteous gift.

The physical law of gravity and other laws which He instituted would give order to the physical world He created. God created mankind to know His love and grace according to our choice. Within the earth that God created would be the discoverable resources of all those things we enjoy today.

From the beginning mankind was given CHOICES concerning THEIR SPIRITUAL RESOLVE, whether to love or hate, do good or evil, make selfish CHOICES; we were not created robots.

God from the beginning sought out Adam and Eve when they chose to go their way and disobey. They hid themselves and were naked and afraid. Before they left the garden God exchanged their covering of leaves for animal skins, a covenant of blood and promise. We still hide and find ourselves naked and broken from the inside out as we run from God's plan for us, in order to control our own lives.

The Scriptures refer to our self-determination and God "be damned" mentality as sin. We by choice come short of God's plan and His best for us. Because of mankind's failure to receive His plan by choice, God made a covenant for our redemption.

From PROMISE TO FULFILMENT we now look to JESUS alone the AUTHOR and FINISHER of our FAITH, CHOOSING GOD'S PROVISION RATHER THAN OUR PERFORMANCE, TRUSTING HIS WORD, HIS WAY AND HIS LIFE. AMAZING GRACE HOW SWEET THE SOUND THAT SAVED A WRETCH LIKE ME.

Finally, Church is not somewhere we go, but rather who we are "in Christ." Going to church meetings does not provide our salvation. God's love and grace at the cross made payment for all our sin.

Today there are hundreds of groups under different names, often claiming to be the only one with the truth. Many split off of others, because of methods, personalities and differing shades of doctrine. Multitudes travel under the same name with an added word to declare their point of difference. Many speak of their church, their pastor and their programs as if possessing the only way, creating a team spirit.

Across America every shopping center and every part of town has buildings and properties labeled church. The Scripture clearly declares that,

> *"The God who made the world and all things in it, since He is Lord of heaven and earth, does not dwell in temples made with hands."*

Finally, the true house of God or temple of God is clearly revealed in Scripture,

> *"...Do you not know that your body is a temple (God's house) of the Holy Spirit who is in you, whom you have from God, and that you are not your own?"*

The truth is that we as believers in the death, burial and resurrection of Jesus Christ are "God's House," bought with a price. We as his people simply gather and scatter, but always "God's House"! He died for us to live in us, to work thru us! Christ in us the hope of glory! CHOOSE GOD'S PROVISION!

CLOSET POWER

Jesus declared,

> "...when you pray, GO INTO YOUR CLOSET, and close the door and pray to your Father who is in secret, and your Father who sees what is done in secret will reward you."

Scripture declares,

> "...the Spirit helps our weakness; for we do not know how to pray as we should, but the Spirit Himself intercedes for us with groanings too deep for words...,"

> "Pray without ceasing."

Jesus Christ came to seek and find us while we were yet sinners, dead in trespasses and sin. He came to die for us, to live in us and to use us for His glory and our good.

In a world of talking heads and faceless crowds, the world of religion has become a consumer item. It's leadership has often become CEO minded rather than servant driven. The life of faith is one of "Closet Power," and "Christ in us the hope of glory." The world of religion often develops a cosmetic plastic piety, overdosed on meeting attending and sermon sampling.

Jesus Christ came to reveal God's love for all mankind without partiality. He came to seek and to save the lost, least and lonely offering His righteousness as a gift of love and grace.

Jesus death, burial and resurrection is the heart of the gospel of grace. He calls us to a life of humility and "Closet Power"! Jesus did not come to start a mass movement or win the world to Himself by corporate gimmicks and appeals.

God throughout human history chose to use His power in one man or woman, to address the world. Masses have indeed come to the simple message of the cross and resurrection, but discipleship demands a walk, up-close and personal.

Jesus Christ always attached Himself to individuals revealing Himself in such a way that each human encounter builds a personal relationship.

We are never commanded to go to church but instructed in how to be the church. The true symbol of Jesus was the towel and the wash bowl as He washed the feet of His disciples exampling the humble servant. Jesus declared,

> *"They will know that you are my disciples because you love one another."*

Anothering is the application of "agapé love" that is unconditional love that reaches out to the brokenness of believer and unbeliever alike, as they are drawn by the Holy Spirit. It is through "Prayer Power" that the believer is empowered. Thus Christianity and its many differing beliefs and dogmas often prove a turn off.

When we follow Jesus in the Scriptures we discover a different Jesus.

Paul declares that,

> *"we should make it our ambition to live a quiet life, mind our own business and work with our hands."*

Peter declares that we should,

> *"sanctify the Lord in our hearts and be ready to give a reason of our hope to THOSE WHO ASK…!"*

THUS BEING CAREFUL TO MAINTAIN GOOD WORKS, FOR THEY ARE GOOD AND PROFITABLE FOR MANKIND. LET OUR LIGHT SO SHINE AMONG MANKIND THAT THEY WILL SEE OUR GOOD WORKS AND GLORIFY OUR FATHER WHICH IS IN HEAVEN.

CONDUIT

A CONDUIT DOES NOT COMMAND WHAT PASSES THROUGH IT, BUT IS A SERVANT TO THE ONE WHO CONTROLS ITS CONTENT!

Growing up religious found me daily playing a game with "Do and Don't Do." At the end of the day my performance score was zero. Then I would prop my guilt up with "I know I am as good as this one or that one." My father taught me that life is about who we really are, not about pretense or appearance. Yet I experienced so many pious religious types who judged me with expectations I couldn't fulfill.

At sixteen I was blessed to encounter others who were struggling with what was true and what was false. I became involved with those who had a love for Jesus without pretense. They became CONDUITS without the COMMANDER mind set filled with judgment which confused my mind. Their behavior was filled with love, grace and compassion without being self-righteous. There was no perfection but a humility that manifested God's love and forgiveness without judgment.

The CONDUIT lifestyle allowed the LIGHT OF CHRIST to manifest itself in shoe leather without the pointed finger or the wagging tongue. Listening ears often reveal more love and grace than any other medium of conversation. Jesus revealed His eternal glory by being real and human, loving broken people. His love manifested compassion unknown to the humanity of man alone. Truly He was humanity untarnished and deity undiminished. Thus He stands alone as THE LAMB OF GOD WHO TOOK ON HIMSELF THE SIN OF THE WORLD BY HIS DEATH, BURIAL AND RESURRECTION.

Thus as CONDUITS we allow His love, His grace and His truth to flow unhindered through us. We do not add our twist and turns to make it work, no self-centered creativity needed, only by His Spirit in us. Our faithfulness to Him will open and close doors as He wills and we are available. Being a COMMANDER becomes more about our performance instead of His provision.

A CONDUIT is a controlled usable vessel filled with His substance under His control.

Scripture declares,

> *"Be not drunk with wine but be filled with the Spirit."*

Doing the work of GOD, Jesus said, was to believe Him whom God sent. As BELIEVER/CONDUITS God can change OUR world as He works in and through us to His glory and our good. Thus THE COMMANDER MIND SET IS ABOUT OUR PERFORMANCE WHEREAS THE CONDUIT LIFESTYLE IS ABOUT GOD'S PROVISION! JESUS DECLARED,

> *"I AM THE WAY, THE TRUTH AND THE LIFE, NO MAN COMES TO THE FATHER BUT BY ME"!*

JESUS WAS GOD'S CONDUIT BY WHICH HE EXPLAINED GOD. WE ARE A CONDUIT OF "CHRIST IN US THE HOPE OF GLORY."

CONSEQUENCES!

Friendships and relationships have CONSEQUENCES that can be joyful or painful. The process of living life as a realist and a pilgrim dealing daily with life situations can lead to wonderful surprises or terrible disappointments. Those who have been a disappointment to me over the years have been persons whom I trusted most.

Someone has said,

> *"Those friends who will dance with you in the rain will likely walk with you in the storm,"*

but not always.

Expectations among friends can be painful when one banks on their love without judgment and it doesn't happen. Disconnecting from a friend because they do not see or say things exactly as you is to reveal the truth about the quality of the relationship in the first place. There is no room for self-righteousness in the believer.

The marriage relationship also brings new tradeoffs and questions. Not just "is this person right for me?" but the greater and most essential question, "Am I the best for him or her and will they be able to tolerate and endure who I am." The leave and cleave factor will test the true character of that relationship and its resulting CONSEQUENCES!

A few years ago I read about a seminary professor who was a brilliant teacher, seminary professor and writer. I read his book about marriage "MEANT TO LAST." Weeks later I read that his wife had left him. I was hurt for him but did not cease reading his books and honoring his gifts as a believer. Things happen to all of us but it does not diminish God's Grace or our usefulness as we repent, confess and rebound.

A few years ago a dear brother in the Lord and a college president, after an affair, married a student. He paid a great price, but like David of old with a contrite heart he continued to love and serve God.

Just out of college I served on a ministry staff where the senior pastor shortly after I arrived had an affair, divorced his wife and married the lady. He wrote me a letter after moving to another ministry in another state repenting of his moral failure and his desire to serve the Lord. He continued to minister faithfully till he died. The CONSEQUENCES were agonizing and painful but in each case there came a renewed resolve to serve God with a broken heart.

Men like David and Solomon who God used to give us wonderful Scriptures that address our daily walk, were men like us flawed and broken. David's adultery and murder and Solomon's excesses included 700 wives, 300 concubines and unacceptable political connections. Their sinful, rebellious acts had major CONSEQUENCES. God uses imperfect people like us to reach out to the least, the lost and the lonely. He does not hide our sinfulness but reveals and forgives it to give hope through His love and grace.

It is called REDEMPTION OFFERED BECAUSE OF MANKIND'S SIN AND BROKENNESS! Often believers harshly judge other believers instead of bearing one another's burdens restoring them and loving them through the CONSEQUENCES of their actions, fulfilling THE LAW OF CHRIST.

It was Forrest Gump who said,

> *"Mama said life is like a box of chocolates; you don't know what's in it until you bite into one."*

INDEED! The ultimate CONSEQUENCES of all of God's love and grace are the "gift of His righteousness," in EXCHANGE for our sin and brokenness.

I rejoice in the fact that God found me and gave me His love and grace. He continues daily dealing with the CONSEQUENCES of my sin and guilt speaking to me from PSALMS AND PROVERBS penned by broken men like me.

Sin of any kind is unacceptable and there are none righteous BUT GOD'S GRACE IS GREATER THAN ALL OUR SIN AS WE TRUST HIM, THE AUTHOR AND FINISHER OF OUR FAITH, and REBOUNDING DAILY.

My Dad, a pastor for 65 years, said before he died that the best years of his life and ministry were between 70 and 90 for he no longer was impressed with anyone and wasn't trying to impress anyone but was just being himself, to God's glory and good.

I HAVE ARRIVED THERE NOW! WALKING IN GOD'S TRUTH, HE BECOMES OUR WISDOM AND VICTORY AS WE FACE THE CONSEQUENCES OF OUR BROKENESS IN JESUS NAME.

AMERICAN EXPERIENCE!

Tim, my son, was a member of the 212th Congress of the United States, a member of the House of Representatives and also a Lieutenant Colonel in the army reserves. I am glad to be an American and am grateful for this land that has nurtured me and offered so many opportunities over the years.

It was in the early 70's that Carolina Christian Day School began "Tour America" with the intent of taking students on sites of the American story and teach it's meaning first hand, up close and personal. It all began when I went to Boston for a wedding at the Harvard University Chapel. While there Tim and I traveled to Plymouth, Lexington, Concord and the Boston area. Out of that exciting trip came the determination to return adding Williamsburg, Jamestown, Yorktown, New York City, Philadelphia and Washington DC. Thus, the senior trip at Carolina Christian Day School became our first Tour America.

When I moved to Arkansas in 1980, Tim and I introduced the Tour America ministry to the youth of Magnolia, Arkansas. The rest is history. We sold BBQ, washed cars and did many different chores earning the money to make the trip a reality. We outfitted a 16 passenger Dodge van with a carry rack on its roof and then contacted churches at all the places we were to travel and secured permission to spend the night in their facilities. I remember the excitement of the youth as they discovered both the beauty and greatness of This Land/Our Land!

I was reminded of this when I returned from standing in the Capitol and Tim being sworn into Congress on my Dad's Bible, visiting his office and the plaque declaring, "Tim Griffin/House of Representatives." The memories are of my trips to India and staying with Tim, a student at Oxford in England and then Tulane Law School and our fun in New Orleans. He then served in the White House as Director of Political Affairs and personal counsel to George Bush.

I have been impressed with his growth, his wedding, his beautiful wife and now his children. I watched him run his campaign in Arkansas for Lieutenant Governor of Arkansas and was impressed by his positive, straight forward approach, refusing to answer his critics and attack his opponents. He stayed on course and defined the issues with conviction. All these memories have walked through my mind these past days as we struggle now with the daily "political war." WE MUST PRAY FOR OURSELVES, EACH OTHER, OUR LEADERSHIP AND THIS NATION!

God has always honored a remnant of people who would honor Him and allow His glory to stand above everything else. We must PRAY WITHOUT CEASING!

America is not a Christian nation, but a nation of Christians; that is a nation of those who have trusted in Jesus Christ the way, the truth and the life. It is this remnant that God blesses and will continue to bless. John Burke said,

> "all evil has to do to triumph is for good men to do nothing"

and an old sage declared

> "that it is better to light one candle than to curse the dark."

Solomon declared,

> "Righteousness exalts a nation and sin is a reproach to any people."

The need is great and we must pray more, complain less, listen more and talk less, seizing the opportunity to declare God's love and we who believe God must be careful to maintain good deeds with great humility for these are good and profitable unto men, that they may see our good works and glorify our Father which is in heaven.

Scripture declares

"I exhort therefore, that first of all, supplications, prayers, intercessions, and giving of thanks, be made for all men; for kings, and for all that are in authority; that we may lead a quiet and peaceable life in all godliness and honesty. For this is good and acceptable in the sight of God our Savior; who will have all men to be saved, and to come unto the knowledge of the truth."

PRAY DAILY AND WITHOUT CEASING!

THE POWER OF ONE

Time and again I have pondered the power of one because our relationship to God and man boils down to a one to one relationship not a corporate production. The measure of salt is not by the beauty of the salt shaker but by the power of each grain bringing flavor to all we encounter. Light is not for a gathering of light fixtures but a scattering of the light within individuals into a dark world. All gathering is for fellowship, accountability and from that huddle to the daily line of scrimmage.

We gather for encouragement centered in the Word of God then back to the world to be light and salt. We don't just go to church; we are the church in a dark and hurting world. Every one plus God is a majority in our generation. God alone keeps the score and totes the note.

God's math is one plus one equals one. We as believers have a great legacy of love and grace in our behalf, and none of it is about us, but HIM. Scripture declares,

> *"No ONE has seen GOD at any time; the only begotten GOD who is in the bosom of the FATHER, HE (Jesus Christ) has explained Him."*

Because this is so we have HIS power in us to "will and to do His good pleasure."

We have the capacity driven by the Holy Spirit to speak God's Word which will impregnate the natural man with the ability to respond to God's gift of righteousness and salvation. It is the Holy Spirit alone who prepares mankind to receive the message of the good news, of Christ's death, burial and resurrection.

We become a part of God's redemptive process as ONE in someone else's life, whether through prayer, a personal word or work of grace, but it is always GOD who gives the increase, or result.

Thus the ONE that we are "in process" is actually "CHRIST in us the hope of glory" not our fleshly editing or testimony that addresses the human heart, but only "the sperm of God's eternal Word." God does not honor us, but His empowering, impregnating Word.

> *"FAITH cometh by hearing and hearing by the "WORD OF GOD"- period.*

Until we surrender our ONE for God's ONE we will keep manipulating people with guilt and fleshly approaches of persuasion and salesmanship getting people to respond temporarily, but never realizing the joy of true faith in the Lord Jesus Christ.

Therefore we produce a religion of do and don't instead of "Amazing Grace" produced by the "done" and completed work of Christ's death, His burial and resurrection. The Scriptures are filled with stories about how God used one person empowered with truth. On the other hand, there have been men and women filled with great wickedness who have changed the world for evil.

We today, stand amidst much change and confusion. We have a great opportunity to affect the lives of those around us daily. As Jesus, the "Power of One" depends on us being clothed with humility and a sense of God's righteousness not our own.

Authenticity means that we stand in authority greater than ours, and not be given to argument and debate, not "wrangling over words to the ruin of the hearer."

Wisdom demands that we lean not on our own understanding, but

> "Trust in the Lord with all our heart."

The wisdom of men puts too much trust in human knowledge and reason.

> *"The natural man does not understand the things of God, nor can he."*

The religious person is so bound to their self-righteousness, forms and traditions that they become blind to the "simplicity which is in Christ." The power of One depends on my favorite Scripture which Paul stated with such majesty and clarity in Romans as follows:

> *"Oh the depth of the riches both of the wisdom and knowledge of God! How unsearchable are His Judgments and unfathomable His ways! For who has known the mind of the Lord, or who became His counselor? Or who has first given to Him that it might be paid back to him again? FOR FROM HIM, AND THROUGH HIM AND TO HIM BE THE GLORY FOREVER."* Amen!

"ONE anothering" reveals OUR MATURITY! The power of one is not only about each of us becoming the best ONE we can be as we grow in grace and knowledge but learning to fulfill the "anothering" as we reach out to other believers in their walk. Many believers have not been taught the tremendous command and blessing to be found in the wonderful joy of "ONE ANOTHERING"!

Be devoted to ONE another…
Give preference to ONE another…

Be of the same mind toward ONE another...
Love ONE another
Accept ONE another...
Admonish ONE another...
Care for ONE another...
Serve ONE another...
Bear ONE another's burdens...
Show patience to ONE another...
Be kind to ONE another...
Do not lie to ONE another...
Bear with ONE another...
Teach and admonish ONE another...
Comfort ONE another...
Encourage ONE another...
Stimulate ONE another to love and good deeds...
Pray for ONE another...
Do not speak against ONE another...
Do not complain...against ONE another...
Clothe yourselves with HUMLITY toward ONE another...

"SANCTIFY THEM IN THE TRUTH; YOUR WORD IS TRUTH." ...THAT THEY MAY ALL BE ONE..." JESUS' HIGH PRIESTLY PRAYER - JOHN 17

Christ in us equals a one that can make a difference in the real world as we translate our faith into a living message without pretense. Being real, being spiritual in natural things and natural in spiritual things, so that

"our light shines before mankind, so that they see our

good works and glorify the Father which is in heaven."

We must moment by moment learn, over a lifetime to allow our one, to yield to His oneness in us, the "hope of glory." Every person is obedient to some reality in their life, even if their obedience is to their own skewed self-centered values.

Obedience to God's authority in our lives is the only real source of meaning and joy. The natural man structures his/her life around themselves, their pleasures and their desires. Thus, there is a power of evil which one can spread and increase its influence by deceit and corruption. The power of THE ONE glows from the inside out driven by God's love and grace, HE CHOSE US IN CHRIST JESUS!

AMBASSADOR

An Ambassador represents one person in the face of another. In another time it was one in behalf of a king representing that king's concerns before another king. In our time it is one who represents a government before another government. As a believer in Jesus Christ I represent His cause daily before my world. Therefore I am given a daily opportunity to declare GOD'S LOVE AND GRACE before a broken and sometimes hostile world.

We are declaring the GOOD NEWS of the cross upon which all our sin was nailed. At the foot of the cross the ground is level. There is no room for pride or arrogance. We all come to the cross as equals broken and undone. It is the ultimate CONTRADICTION to our self-righteousness. Thus, each believer is an AMBASSADOR!

Before Paul was as apostle of Jesus Christ he was Saul the bounty hunter. He sought out believers to kill them and remove them. After his life changing experience on the Damascus road he was devoted to the Lord Jesus Christ as a bond servant. He faithfully proclaimed the GOOD NEWS of Jesus death, burial and resurrection! His forever resume was Chief of Sinners, Least of the Apostles and a Nobody!

Paul certainly would not be found acceptable to our success motivated religious culture today as he finished his years in a Roman prison and finally died under the cruel hand of Nero! The call of God on every believer is not pastor, teacher, missionary or prophet, but WITNESS! A WITNESS is not judge or jury but one who has been found by GOD'S ETERNAL LOVE AND GRACE AND RECEIVED IT BY FAITH! A joy beyond measure!

It is not a "religious thing" but a redemptive matter not based on human performance but GOD'S provision! Jesus death on the cross and his burial and resurrection are GOOD NEWS!

Every believer is given a measure of faith and grace by which God's righteousness is freely given to all who trust Him. With that salvation each believer is graced with "gifts of the Spirit" by which to serve other believers! Truly "CHRIST IN YOU THE HOPE OF GLORY!"

There are many ways to give witness to our great salvation. Each individual brings to his or her WITNESS the special authentication of their character and personality. We learn to be there for others, "bearing their burdens" with more listening than talk until they request "the hope within us."

As conduits of God's love and grace we must ever realize that as conduits it is not us but the WITNESS MESSAGE inside the conduit! FAITH COMES BY HEARING AND HEARING BY THE WORD OF GOD.

Finally, we each must allow the HOLY SPIRIT to guide us into all TRUTH! The genius of our personal WITNESS can be best expressed by our being REAL and AVAILABLE without judging and self-righteousness, as we manifest great love for broken people, the least, the lost and the lonely.

These days after years of reading and owning a large library I have realized that my greatest opportunity for reaching out is with my pen believing that indeed THE PEN IS GREATER THAN THE SWORD, thus leaving behind a residue of my WITNESS after I am gone to heaven!

A BLOGGER CONFRONTS LIFE'S CHOICES!

Though we all are different we still example similar behaviors. Our daily routines are our greatest challenge. My life journey set its compass with JESUS CHRIST as my true north years ago. My routine has often been broken and upset by life choices made out of selfishness or expectations that failed. My spiritual warfare begins each day when I awake. Our faith journey is common to all thus our greatest victories and our greatest defeats are to be found in the daily ROUTINE of life.

As new believers we should have been taught about the war in the ordinary where God's provision is far greater than our performance! We have no righteousness but GOD'S and it is a gift. Thus, life by its nature is often complex and out of balance. The wisdom of Scriptures and work of the Holy Spirit in each believer's life renews our inner man moment by moment as we practice HIS presence. Life's ROUTINE has many demands and we also draw strength from others who share our common struggle as believers in God's love and grace.

From birth to our death we are on a JOURNEY. No one will ever preach our funeral for we are preaching our own daily. Each of us is a special one of a kind.

Every thought, activity and routine forms our way of thinking and living. Thus, all of us are a product of the good, the bad and the ugly. We had to be taught or programmed to hate. Loving and caring for others can be exampled, but because of our sinful nature we must have an encounter with that which is greater than our selfish nature.

Early in my journey I was introduced to religion and morality by laws and rules. They whitewashed my life so I could act a part that wasn't really mine. I was like the little lizard that turned the color of whatever it landed on. The easy way of becoming what others want us to be tempts us all from time to time. At 16 years of age Jesus ceased being a lawyer and judge to me, but a loving Savior. Weary of religion I found great peace and rest in JESUS CHRIST, HIS DEATH ON THE CROSS AND HIS RESURRECTION!

THIS BLOGGER'S HOPE CHEST

SEARCH of SCRIPTURE:

(1) To discover the nature and character of GOD!

(2) To know who we are because of who GOD is!

(3) To define error because many things said to be true about God and Scripture are false!

(4) To discern Birth Truth from Growth Truth.

BELIEVERS ASSURANCE POLICY

1 JOHN 3:1-3:

> *"See what kind of love the FATHER has given to us that we should be called children of GOD, and so we are."*

The reason why the world does not know us is that it did not know HIM.

> *"Beloved, we are GOD'S children now and what we will be has not yet appeared; but we know that when HE appears we shall be like HIM, because we shall see HIM as he is. And everyone who thus HOPES in HIM purifies himself as HE is pure."*

ABSENT FROM THE BODY PRESENT WITH THE LORD, CHOOSE THIS DAY WHOM YOU WILL SERVE!

SO-BE-IT

"Multitudes of Christians within the church are moving toward the point where they reject the institution that we call the church. They are beginning to turn to more simplified forms of worship. They are hungry for a personal and vital experience with Jesus Christ."

Billy Graham
World Aflame (Crusade Edition)

OTHER WORKS BY DANNY GRIFFIN

- **<u>Dancing With Broken Feet</u>**
  Dealing with the pain and pressures of marriage including divorce, remarriage, blended families and more

- **<u>Living Waters, Empty Wells and Holy Dippers</u>**
  Danny's work in India

- **<u>Born To War</u>**
  From birth to maturity of the believer

- **<u>For Those Who Ask</u>**
  Ambassadorial evangelism

- **<u>I Must Say</u>**
  A poetic parody by Ismael Footfahrt

- **<u>Freedom Drive</u>**
  The story of Carolina Christian Ministries, day school, fellowship and how it came to be

- **<u>Her!</u>**
  Thoughts on love, romance and intimacy in poetic form

For information on how to obtain any of the above visit:
<u>http://www.SpiritualMaintenance.org/Books.html</u>